Beowulf: A Likeness

Beowulf: A Likeness

Randolph Swearer
Raymond Oliver
Marijane Osborn

Introduction by Fred C. Robinson

Yale University Press
New Haven and London

Published with the assistance of the Joukowsky Family Fund
and the National Endowment for the Arts

Designed by Randolph Swearer
Set in Bembo and Univers type by Highwood Typographic Services,
Hamden, Connecticut
Printed in the United States of America by Rembrandt Printing, Inc.,
Woodbridge, Connecticut.

Library of Congress Cataloging-in-Publication Data
Swearer, Randolph.
Beowulf: a likeness / Randolph Swearer, Raymond Oliver, Marijane
Osborn; introduction by Fred C. Robinson.
     p. cm.
ISBN 0-300-04876-9 (alk. paper)
1. Beowulf. 2. Beowulf—Adaptations. 3. Epic poetry, English (Old)—
Modernized versions. 4. Epic poetry, English (Old)—History and criticism.
I. Oliver, Raymond, 1936– . II. Osborn, Marijane. III. Title.
PR1585.S94 1990
829'.3—dc2O   90-34386
                                                      CIP

The paper in this book meets the guidelines for permanence and
durability of the Committee on Production Guidelines for Book Longevity
of the Council on Library Resources.

10 9 8 7 6 5 4 3 2 1

Contents

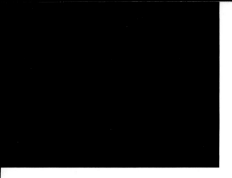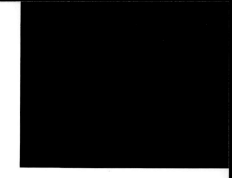

Preface and Acknowledgments

This volume tells the story of *Beowulf*. It also meditates on and explores the poem's silences—those aspects that, owing to the passage of time, appear to the modern reader as dim reflections of a deeper reality—but it does not seek to explain them away.

My aim in the design has been neither to imitate nor to illustrate *Beowulf*, but rather, through imagery suggested by the fragments of tribal history, geography, and material culture preserved in the poem, to offer broad structural analogies for the path and rhythms of the story. Yet by definition design does not function in isolation, and the visual aspects of this volume should not be considered apart from the contributions of my collaborators.

Indeed, one of the most rewarding aspects of my role has been bringing together an extraordinary group of people to focus their talents on this powerful tale. Fred Robinson, who helped me in fundamental ways during the development of this project, inspired important aspects of the design. Raymond Oliver lent his thoughtful support, and above all contributed his innovative version of *Beowulf*, which lies at the heart of this volume. I owe much to Marijane Osborn, who rekindled my interest in *Beowulf* with her fine translation and later guided me on a Migration Period adventure through the swamps of the Leire countryside and onto the crags of Fjällbacka. If our collaboration has succeeded, we have left resonant silences of our own that respond to those in the original tale.

Judy Metro, my editor, has helped to shape and nurture this project since its inception. The artistic vision in many of the photographs belongs to Kate Breakey, whose contributions I deeply appreciate. Jan Eckborg in Sweden has always offered his support and warm hospitality, and Pat and Paul Bolwig were kind hosts in Copenhagen. I appreciate the hospitality of and assistance from James Campbell and Terry Hoad at Oxford. I thank Edward Saenz, my production assistant. Many thanks are also due to Jenny Glazebrook and the Sutton Hoo Research Project for allowing us to photograph the site there, and to the Early English Text Society and the British Library for permission to reproduce manuscript pages from *Beowulf*. The Sutton Hoo artifacts are reproduced with the kind permission of the Trustees of the British Museum, and Bagger Rosenkilde generously allowed me to use illustrations from "Wonders of the East." Last, but certainly not least, I owe much to Sarah, who has logged many miles with me in the Beowulfian hinterlands and beyond.

I am grateful for the grants I received for this project from the National Endowment for the Arts, the University Research Institute and the College of Fine Arts Summer Research Fund at The University of Texas at Austin, and the Joukowsky Family Foundation.

Randolph Swearer
Austin, Texas, 1990

Pages from the *Beowulf* manuscript, Cotton
Vitellius A.15, now in the British Library.
The unique shape of this manuscript is the
result of its damage in a fire in AD 1731.

Introduction

Fred C. Robinson

Pound's Cavalcanti: An Edition of the Translations, Notes, and Essays, ed. David Anderson (Princeton, 1983), p. 12.

The poet-translator Ezra Pound shrewdly observed that "it is conceivable the poetry of a far-off time or place requires a translation not only of word and spirit, but of 'accompaniment', that is, that the modern audience must in some measure be made aware of the mental content of the older audience, and of what these others drew from certain fashions of thought and speech."* Only the inspired metaphrast of Cavalcanti's poems and of the Old English *Seafarer* could have seen and stated so clearly this problem in re-creating an ancient masterpiece for modern English readers. The verbal content of a work can be Englished, but the resultant translation exists in a cultural vacuum. The antique world of Homer or of Vergil or of the *Beowulf* poet having vanished, the old poems' tone and allusions and literary effects echo through a cultural void and lose their meanings. The translated text may be read, but it no longer connects with its audience. Traditionally scholars and translators have sought to overcome this loss of context by surrounding the translated poem with a matrix of footnotes and commentary which attempt to reassemble the work's original cultural milieu, in so far as that milieu is recoverable through primary and secondary sources. But the dry notes of scholarship are so remote in tone and intention from the text they seek to revivify that the two do not cohere into a meaningful aesthetic experience. What is needed, as Pound rightly says, is a translated "accompaniment," something that harmonizes with the ancient poetry and helps to complete its meaning.

This volume is a rendition of the Old English heroic poem *Beowulf* with an accompaniment. The original poem, often called the primary epic of the English language, was composed some time during the Anglo-Saxon period (AD 449–1066) from subject matter and in a traditional style which originated in the continental homeland of the English before they migrated from northern Europe and founded on the island of Britain what came to be the English nation. We do not know who the author was or where in England he lived, but his poem is eloquently expressive of the culture which produced it, and its details and nuances resonate with much else that survives from Anglo-Saxon England—other literature, artwork, archaeological remains, and reconstructible history—as well as with legendary and historical analogues from other Germanic cultures.

It is from this broad cultural context, imaginatively apprehended, that the accompaniment here presented derives. The book's design and the commentary on it provide a unique visual complement to Raymond Oliver's poem, which is a re-creation (with its own built-in accompaniment) of the ancient tale of *Beowulf* using modern verse forms. The product of wide travels and deep reflection on the poem by photographer-designer Randolph Swearer, the images are intercallated with the narrative in such a way as to prompt the eye with relevantly evocative displays as the mind contemplates the details of the old legend. In a sense they provide the words of the poem with a visual world in which to come alive, somewhat as gesture animates speech. This volume is not designed page-by-page but as two-page units, and the reader should see the images and the segment of text presented at any opening of the book as a meaningful unit. As in the narrative poem itself, there is a sustained linearity in the arrangement of the images, with visual themes being developed, relinquished, and resumed as the story's events unfold stage by stage: the hero's sea-journey, entering the hall, the haunted mere—each segment of the narrative has its own pictorial development. At times a sequence of images explores spaces and perspectives in the legend of *Beowulf*: outdoors and indoors, seeing out from within, peering in from without, scenes and events contained in memory. At times a sequence suggests a sense of place or of history, at other times a mood. Although carefully coordinated with the movement of Oliver's poem, the images are not interdependent with the words. The two are simultaneous and intersinuate meditations on an ancient masterpiece.

Previous books have provided *Beowulf* with photographic *illustrations,* but such a use of photography is limited. An archaeologist's photograph of the rusted, skeletal remains of an Anglo-Saxon sword does not summon to mind what a sword looked like to an eighth-century Englishman or what it meant to him. And so Swearer offers instead a modern artist-photographer's poetic conception of ancient Germanic scenes and artifacts. The helmets and landscapes and posthole patterns and manuscript leaves shimmer in strange lighting or fade from view in ways suggestive of the olden time we seek to retrieve when we contemplate the story of *Beowulf.* Especially important are the frequently appearing reproductions of the *Beowulf* manuscript, whether in sharp detail or shadowy backdrop. These provide a constant reminder of the fragile, antique document upon which all in this book is ultimately based, and of the fact that the poem presented here is a *likeness* of something old and elusive.

While the images are at times oblique and suggestive, they are not intended to be puzzling. Therefore Marijane Osborn has provided a commentary which explains what readers are encountering when they turn to any given page, and at times she deepens our appreciation of a passage or image by supplying further relevant information drawn from her unique store of knowledge about Old English poetry and Anglo-Saxon and Scandinavian antiquities, as well as from her travels through the lands and waterways of Scandinavia, retracing the routes followed by Beowulf and his contemporaries. Her acquaintance with the scenes and artifacts of the North is so intimate and extensive that one can only admire the selection and restraint which give her commentary its accessibility and utility. The photograph of the bog in the outdoor museum near Leire (pages 22–23) has the graphic force of a sharp Dürer etching and is sufficiently eerie to set the scene for the strange events that occur at Hart (Old English *Heorot*). But buried in the volumes on a medieval scholar's shelf are important details which link the scene and the story in many important ways. Chronicles and histories and sagas from early Scandinavia identify Leire as the very town where the ancient kings of the Danes had their royal halls—their Hart. And an even earlier source, the Roman historian Tacitus, tells us that the ancient Germans used bogs for places of execution, submerging those who were guilty of crimes of shame, such as cowardice, in the marshy soil, expunging their very memories from the tribal mind. And a medieval German chronicler named Thietmar of Merseburg tells us that at Leire in January of every ninth year the pagan Danes sacrificed ninety-nine men and the same number of various species of animals to the gods. With tact and deft economy Osborn tells us just enough of all this history and legend to establish the vital connections between the bog scene, Hart, and the pagan sacrifices of the Danes in *Beowulf.* The eerie mood of the photographic image is deepened by this history, and its link to the story of Beowulf is reinforced. While her commentary illuminates the book's design and validates

Oliver's accompaniment to the old story he is telling, it is more than ancillary. The commentary assembles out of the scholar's plenty of fact and legend and long studied antiquities her own imaginative reconstruction of the story of Beowulf in its native setting. Poem, design, and commentary are mutually enriched without losing their integrity.

In the preface to his poem Raymond Oliver is careful to emphasize that *Beowulf: A Likeness* is in no sense a translation of the Old English poem but rather "an interpretation in verse of *Beowulf.*" Ezra Pound might have described it as a rendering of the word and spirit of the poem with an accompaniment, for the "adding, subtracting and rearranging" that Oliver speaks of is clearly intended to make readers aware, as Pound says, "of the mental content of the older audience." It may be useful to consider some of the ways in which Oliver's changes do, paradoxically, bring us closer to a contemporary Anglo-Saxon's experience of the poem *Beowulf* than would a bare-bones literal translation.

The Old English poem begins with a twenty-five line prelude tracing the origins of the Danish royal dynasty before, in lines 26–52, the death and funeral of King Scyld are impressively described. Modern scholars have pointed out that the *Beowulf* poet's special fondness for balance, contrast, and envelope patterns makes it likely that the funeral in lines 26–52 and Beowulf's funeral described at the close of the poem are intended to frame the narrative with images of death and grief, an apt reminder of "this brief tragedy of flesh" which would have been more immediately apparent to a practiced Anglo-Saxon audience than it is to most modern readers. Oliver has effectively accentuated this framing device simply by shifting Scyld's death to the opening line of the poem:

> When Scyld the distant-father died of time . . .

and by adding at the end of the poem an epitaph reminding us that all great men must "die of time."

The portrait of the character named Wulf near the beginning of Oliver's poem is his invention pure and simple, but its sources are easily recognizable—snaggly-toothed skulls unearthed by Anglo-Saxon archaeologists, descriptions of boisterous feasts in Old Norse sagas and in Saxo Grammaticus's *Gesta Danorum,* and perhaps the amazingly well preserved body of Lindow man recently recovered from an English bog. The grainy depiction of Wulf, who is a kind of Every-thane, is an important corrective to most modern readers' anachronistically refined conception of the Germanic warriors in *Beowulf.* It also enables us to experience more poignantly the shock and horror of Grendel's initial attack on the Danes when we are told that the monster's first victim was the amiable, earthy Wulf, whom we had come to know at first hand.

Another of Oliver's additions is in a later account of Grendel's attacks:

> Often, as if to claim it, as he fled

> He dropped his dung along the floor, its stench
> Worse than a hundred rotting hogs in summer.

Besides concretizing the loathesomeness of the monster, this detail highlights his animal nature, an important aspect of a creature who is presented as a mixture of man, brute, and demon.

Again, when Hrothgar and his men come to the rim of the ghastly tarn where Grendel's enraged mother lies waiting for any human being who will challenge her,

> They saw a pool as dead and grey as stone.
> All stood together; each man felt alone.

There is no basis for this in the Old English poem, but for me Oliver's couplet captures precisely the mood of that instant by the tarn.

Elsewhere a phrase or added detail brings out the dry humor of a passage in *Beowulf,* since the Old English poet's humor is so understated and sardonic that modern readers often miss it altogether. The remark in the original poem (lines 138–42) that many Danes spent the night in remote cabins after Grendel began terrorizing the great hall has an undertone of mild derision which is well defined by Oliver's embellishment:

> Many Danes
> Began to think festivities at Hart
> Might be improved and life less fraught with strain
> If things weren't quite so crowded.

The sarcasm of the exchange between Beowulf and Unferth often seems subtler to modern ears than was probably intended. The rude taunts in Oliver's version of the exchange restore the abrasive surface of the original.

In one respect Oliver has clarified and rationalized language in *Beowulf* which I believe the poet, for reasons which are perhaps no longer compelling, intended to be subtle and oblique. The terms which characters in the original poem use to refer to divine powers are notably imprecise, so that there has always been some uncertainty among modern readers of *Beowulf* as to whether pagan deities or the Christian God is in question. Any Anglo-Saxon listening to *Beowulf* would have known that the hero and all the other characters in the poem had to be heathens who were loyal to the only deities they knew—the Germanic pantheon of Woden, Tiw, and the other northern gods. Indeed, the poet tells us early in the narrative that the Danes, in their desperation over Grendel's attacks, make sacrifices to pagan gods. But living in a devoutly Christian England in a time when militant Germanic paganism was still a threat to the true faith, the poet could not emphasize this point too much by having his noble Germanic characters call on the pagan gods by name and practice heathen abominations like sortilege and human sacrifice; to do so would have scandalized the clergy and made it impossible for any Christian Englishman to admire and sympathize with the characters in *Beowulf.* Therefore the poet has his characters allude to superior beings in terms which are carefully selected and deliberately vague. *Se ælmihtiga, ealdmetod, wealdend,* and *god,* which mean "the almighty one," "(an) ancient ruler," "(a) wielder," and "(a) god," are the kinds of terms the characters use when they speak of a divine presence. They never use explicitly Christian names of the Deity (Jesus, Savior, Christ, and so on), nor do they shock the Christian audience with names like Woden and Tiw. When speaking in his own voice the poet usually employs more or less general words for the Christian Deity as well, thus minimizing on the surface the contrast between heathen and Christian. When a speaker in the poem says "the almighty one" or "ancient ruler," the referent of the term depends entirely on who the speaker is. If it is the Christian poet, we know that God is the referent; if it is a pagan character, a darker power must be meant. Editors and translators of *Beowulf* have in the past perversely capitalized the initial letter of all these terms, thus making it appear that everyone is speaking of God. This capitalization of letters has no foundation in the original manuscript, and it has led critics and scholars into much confused speculation over the religious faith of the Germanic heroes in the poem. The poet, by his deft selection of terms, leaves it to the audience to infer the religious affiliation of the persons speaking and avoids jarring clashes of belief in the diction of the poem. This studied vagueness of reference also enables the audience to contemplate and even revere their pre-Christian ancestors without compromising their own Christian faith.

The poet's subtlety of reference, which was crucial to the presentation of his story at the theologically complicated time when he was composing *Beowulf,* is not necessary for a modern audience, which even has difficulty understanding the intensity of religious imperatives and anxieties in an earlier age in the West. Therefore Oliver's simplification of the spiritual climate in his poem, where Beowulf and Hrothgar are portrayed as Germanic heroes who had somehow heard a bit about Christianity, frees readers to turn their attention to other matters in the story which would have equal importance for an Anglo-Saxon and a modern audience. And the reader of today can admire Oliver's deeply moving description of the death of Beowulf—

> He spoke no more; his soul was like a place
> Entirely filled with light, nothing but light—
> Wholly empty and wholly full, bright space—
> Or like the same place filled with perfect night.
> He entered now the greater emptiness
> Of death—and greater fullness of God no less—

without concern for the fact that an Anglo-Saxon reader would have been puzzled by the last seven words, since a man wholly ignorant of Christian doctrine could not, according to medieval Christian belief, have encountered God after his death.

Perhaps the most daring departure Oliver has made in his telling of *Beowulf* is his adoption of several modern metrical forms to render the old narrative, which, in its original state, is narrated in traditional Germanic alliterative verse throughout. Many attempts have been made to imitate the old alliterative-accentual meter in modern verse, and they have generally failed because modern ears are not attuned to the intricacies and effects of this long disused prosody. They *are* attuned to the forms Oliver uses, and he calculates with care our responses to the particular forms which he assigns to the various speakers and passages in his poem. The basic six-line stanza which he uses for narrative is that of which Shakespeare made similar use in *Venus and Adonis,* probably having taken it from Thomas Lodge's *Scylla's Metamorphosis,* another long narrative poem. The slightly faster-moving four-stressed lines linked by assonance are a supple measure appropriate to dialogue, while blank verse and heroic couplets are used in passages whose subject matter seems to call for these forms. The six-line stanza and couplets require a good deal of rhyming, and twentieth-century ears accustomed to much free verse and blank verse might find too many chiming words distracting. Oliver therefore introduces off-rhymes like *nations : patience, ditch : fixed,* and *acid : rapid,* which artfully avoid the predictability of the traditional forms and give the ear an occasional rest from rhyme. Also alliteration is used pervasively but with a light touch—a carefully understated reference to the form of the original Old English poem.

The important part that metrical form can play in our perception and enjoyment of poetry is well exemplified in *Beowulf: A Likeness.* The chief pleasure of metered verse is the interplay of form and matter, the sense of events and thoughts and dramatic exchanges being steadily constrained into appropriate order and proportion. The Geatish nation's falling to ruin narrated with a serene metrical fitting together provides a combination of sad disintegration with reassuring evenness of cadence that reminds one of the solemn interplay of meter and matter in the closing scenes of some of Shakespeare's tragedies. In Oliver's narration of Hrethel's death of a broken heart and the epic simile of the father grieving over his hanged son which expresses Hrethel's grief, the seemingly effortless rhymes and rhythms of the six-line stanza contribute more than readers might at first realize to the artist's sublimation of human wretchedness into sweetly moving poetry. And in the exchange between Beowulf and the spiteful Unferth it is the couplet form perfected by Alexander Pope which marks the transformation of mere anger and indignation into icy repartee—as in Pope's

> Yet let me flap this bug with gilded wings,
> This painted child of dirt that stinks and stings.

By displaying so forcefully and variously the ways in which the discipline of meter guides and shapes our apprehension of subject matter, Oliver reminds us of the extent to which that very different but equally disciplined meter of the original Old English *Beowulf* interacts with voice and style and narrative details to create the unique aesthetic experience which it provides.

But the emphasis here on differences between Oliver's poem and the Old English *Beowulf* has perhaps been a little misleading, for the dominant impression one receives from this new verse telling of the old story is one of intimate cooperation with the original text. Echoing throughout *Beowulf: A Likeness* are re-inventions of segments of Old English poetry in modern language and verse: "while still he wielded words," "shadow-shapes of night came on," "he hoped but, wise and old, did not expect that they would meet again," "when swords had drunk of him he died," "bright on the bone his sword had bit more weakly than he could wish," and "as useless now to men as it had always been, it lies buried" are phrases which bring pleasing shocks of recognition to the reader who knows *Beowulf* in the original language, for they are Old English turns of phrase reborn in living modern English verse.

Oliver's poem and the Old English *Beowulf* are most similar in their broad shape and complex tone. Both poems are about a hero sublime in his simplicity. The language of both is rich with imagery. If no modern English verse can quite replicate the pervasive and imbedded imagery of Old English poetic diction, Swearer's design, with its spectrum of haunting images, goes some distance toward making up the difference.† There is much joy in both poems: the animal high spirits in celebrating victories, the exhilaration of lavish feasting and openhanded generosity, the joys of true friendship and manly devotion, and the profound joy at the

†Notice for example how the images on pages 12–13 reify the simile in line 218 of the Old English poem, which says that Beowulf's ship crosses the sea "most like a bird."

end of *Beowulf,* where the hero's death is transcended by his achievement of a life well lived and of the fame which is the reward of such a life. But the joy of the poem is shadowed and often eclipsed by the recurrent melancholy which gives *Beowulf* that tonal complexity which almost defies characterization. The poet's narrative device of interrupting descriptions of triumphant moments with prophecies of disasters to come; the aching sense of the transience of human life which is invoked again and again; and the nostalgic pang of deep loss which one feels when recalling a past era of great events to which one is attached through some special kinship—these elements are present and equally moving in the old Anglo-Saxon poem and in the new poem by Raymond Oliver, which is indeed a likeness of *Beowulf.* Its technical panache, so different in detail from that of the Old English poet,‡ is nonetheless a sound equivalent. Suffused with exultation, nostalgia, death and regret, Oliver's poem glows like its prototype with the bright hues of blood and gold in a surrounding darkness. And along with all its distinctive and traditional literary effects—its echoing formulas, its sounding maxims, its scraps of history and hints at long-remembered legends—it is a strange and moving story, compellingly told and seriously interesting to any serious reader of books.

‡Actually, Oliver has an early Germanic precedent for his tour-de-force telling of *Beowulf* in many different, challenging meters: Snorri Sturlson's *Háttatal,* the third and last part of his *Prose Edda,* is composed in 102 stanzas, each of which illustrates a distinct skaldic verse-form.

Prologue

Raymond Oliver

This is an interpretation in verse of *Beowulf*, a celebration of its meaning and of the crude but rich fund of experience from which it proceeds. In aim and genre *Beowulf: A Likeness* is not unlike the *Morte Darthur* of Sir Thomas Malory, whose treatment of his source, "the French book," involves much adding, subtracting, and rearranging of large structural units as well as a thorough rewording; it can be securely described neither as translation nor "imitation" nor, in our post-Romantic sense, as an original work. Its general class appears to have no name. And though the verse is strict and at times lightly alliterates, it is not alliterative in the old Germanic way. It maintains its principal link with the Anglo-Saxon tradition in being conceived orally, to be read aloud. I have used a variety of meters, all of them accentual-syllabic, because varying the forms allows a closer fit between language and speaker or occasion; thus the harshly ironic words between Beowulf and Unferth are in heroic couplets, the form developed for such purposes by Dryden and Pope.

Beowulf is about a strong and good man, a leader among Germanic tribes of the early sixth century, who accepts three extraordinary challenges, two in his youth and the last in old age. To convey the plot, setting, characters, and so forth, I have tried to adapt the (realistic) techniques of the historical novel in such a way as to support the nonrealism of this old tale. Such an approach has meant assimilating into the text the kind of lore—historical, archaeological, and literary—found in scholarly works about *Beowulf*. The original invites this treatment, since quite often it simply indicates a description or background rather than presenting it, almost as if giving bare stage-directions; and there is little interest in analyzing motives or the impact of events. So quite often I give the description, fill in the background, analyze the characters and events. For instance the *Beowulf* poet does not show us vividly what a mead-hall was like, physically and socially, because he could take for granted this knowledge and therefore a full understanding of the loss Grendel inflicts when he ravages Hart Hall. But none of us have been in a mead-hall, so I have included a Breughelesque picture of Hart early in the poem, drawing—here as elsewhere—on period details from the continent as well as England, sixth through tenth or eleventh centuries (a compromise owing to the sparseness of early Anglo-Norse data). This passage is, so to speak, an expanded gloss on the Old English word "meduseld," mead-hall—a gloss that includes as much historical resonance as possible, ranging from "mentalités" to table-manners. And the same is true of other such passages: their purpose is to present what the original has merely named or implied.

But this poem is neither *Beowulf* nor a faithful translation nor even an attempt at thorough historical reconstruction. The poet is a twentieth-century American, not a sixth-century Scandinavian or an eighth- or tenth-century Anglo-Saxon; and the narrative voice tells the tale with varying degrees of empathy and intimacy with the world of Beowulf, trying to avoid gross anachronism, but not scholarly imperfections of the "coasts of Bohemia" sort. I have written for those who can enjoy narrative in verse—metrical verse at that, and a tale of long ago and far away.

The first page of the *Beowulf* manuscript

HWÆT WE GARDE

na ingear dagum. þeod cyninga
þrym ge frunon huða æþelingas elle
fre medon. oft scyld scefing sceaþe
þreatum moneʒū mæʒþum meodo setl
of teah egsode eorl syððan ærest wear
þea sceaft funden he þæs frofre geba
weox under wolcnum weorð myndum þah
oð þ him æghwylc þara ymb sittendra
ofer hron rade hyran scolde gomban
gyldan þ wæs god cyning. ðæm eafera wæs
æfter cenned geong ingeardum þone god
sende folce tofrofre fyren ðearfe on
geat þ hie ær drugon aldor ase lange
hwile him þæs lif frea wuldres weal de
worold are forgeaf beowulf wæs bren
blæd wide sprang scyldes eafera scede
landum in · Swa sceal
ge wyrcean fromum feoh giftum on fæder

I. In Denmark

i. Grendel

When Scyld the distant-father died of time,
Old in winters, come to the end of deeds,
His body being fresh as in his prime,
Sweet as flowers newly mown in the meads,
They wrapped it all in linen trimmed with gold,
And otter-furs against the snowy cold,

And bore it on a bed of willow-wands
Down to the sea, as he himself had bidden
While still he wielded words though tight in the bonds
Of death; he didn't wish his body hidden
Beneath the dark of dirt. At oceanside
The ring-stem boat turned slowly in a tide

That seemed to wait for Scyld while moving out.
The vessel's skin was lacquer-sheathed in ice;
Seagulls, like messengers, were perched about
On rails and hawk-beak prowhead. Made to slice
Water, the prow was roughly honed; its motion,
A nervous bobbing, pointed to the ocean.

They laid the king amidships by the mast,
The lord they loved, whose gifts of golden rings
They likewise loved; the boat embraced him fast,
As he embraced the countless priceless things
They placed with him: a sword of hammered blade
And jewelled hilt, its grip a golden braid,

A byrnie light and loose as a shining fleece,
Bronze-panelled helms with little beads of jet,
Brooches in cloisonné where every piece
Of millefiori glass or garnet had been set
In thick red gold, a bag of coins, a chest
Of silken garments; all was of the best....

There's never been a boat so well adorned
With treasure, battle-gear, and richest clothes;
The ones who sent him to the ocean scorned
The petty ways of thrift no less than those
Who'd once put Scyld aboard a wherry piled
With gifts, alone on waves and him a child.

Yeavering in northern England;
the site of an important dynastic center
in Anglo-Saxon times.

They set a silken flag above his head,
High on the mast; then bracing shoulders to hull
They heaved through freezing surf, slowly; then sped
Rapidly as the tide took hold. A gull
Rose from the prow. They gave their Scyld away
To the sea; but who received him, none could say.

Long after, Hrothgar woke in the world, the son
Of Scyld's best grandson. He did well in war—
Always he slaughtered many, always won—
And got himself such fame, and such a store
Of treasure, that from every nearby land
Young men arrived; they pressed to join his band.

One day at dawn it entered Hrothgar's mind
That he must have a hall, the greatest hall
That men had known, with gilded roof, designed
And built by masters, where he'd deal out all
To young and old, all goods in his command,
All wealth but other men's and public land.

I heard he brought in men from many nations
To do the work, from all round middle-earth.
Quickly they worked, for Hrothgar was impatient
To have a mead-hall to display his worth.
And so it rose, in every way apart,
Most handsome, highest hall. He named it "Hart."

A stone-bright path, which pierced the outer wall
Of dully pointed logs and crossed the ditch,
Brought you to where the antlers of the hall,
Head with horns of a twelve-point stag they'd fixed
Above the door, showed "Hart" to passers-by
And to the stars and sun; they stood up high

The burial ship, based on a ninth-century ship excavated at Oseberg in Norway, floats over the landscape of Sutton Hoo in East Anglia, the site of a seventh-century Anglo-Saxon ship burial.

Even above the gable, brown on gold.
The timbers, deep in earth and shorn of bark,
Were painted red and yellow, brightly bold
To suit the roof, to light December's dark.
It was like this, a peaceful winter's day
Before the trouble swept all peace away:

Morning, the coast of Denmark, in the year
Four ninety-seven, snow and greyish trees
Frozen in perfect stillness, dark on clear.
The sun is turning vague. This cold will freeze
Not only breath but blood, given the chance;
You feel in fingertips its mute advance,

In spite of sheepskin mittens. Pigs and sheep
Are penned in yards within the palisade;
They move at random. Snow, already deep
On ground and roofs, its settling briefly delayed
By wind, begins again to move in the air,
Lightly. Otherwise nothing; everywhere

The world is still. That pile of logs, a wall
Of whitened black, prolongs by forty feet
Of oak and fir the northern end of the hall,
Making it thick against the snow and sleet
As, turned to fire, it heats the hall within.
Its ghostly smoke is rising twisted, thin.

And Hrothgar didn't lay his boast aside:
Behind this oaken door adorned with nails
And boar's-head handle, Hrothgar did preside,
Giving as from the horn that never fails,
Each night at banquet, gifts to keep—not lent—
To faithful men who followed where he went.

Gold glinted in the hearth- and candle-fire.
That other fire had not yet whelmed the hall,
The one aroused by edge-hate and desire,
Killing of kin that led to final fall.
It was like this for now, a winter's night
Before the nearer trouble came in sight:

A twelve-foot trestle table, planks of oak
Polished only by beer and sweat and sleeves
Of linsey-woolsey. Thick men loosely joke
And jostle; such good humor rarely achieves
The comic. Almost pleasantly they stink,
Like livestock. And especially they drink:

Their Danish wine, like grapejuice cut with acid,
Their grainy, essence-of-a-hayfield beer,
Mead from the scented meads—all downed in rapid
Tankard- or mug- or gobletfuls, good cheer
To slosh the mouth and swell the belly and flush
The skull, warm redness spreading with a rush

The reconstructed Anglo-Saxon village at
West Stow in East Anglia (not far from
Sutton Hoo).

Across the face. One notes the impacts: mug
On table, mead on mood; the stony clay
Thuds on the wood, fomenting liquors drug
The brain. At first in likenesses of play
They prod with words and fingers; someone blames
His friend for nothing; eyes show tiny flames;

At last they slump to silence. That takes hours;
The nights are long. Not all take fire. This night
The thanes had come here from their private bowers
By dark, their ladies clad in rain-grey white
Like lilies seen through mist; they leave outside,
Upright, their grey-tipped spears, and slowly stride

Into the hall, like thunder on the boards.
A kind of dinner-party, but the men
Take spears that little way and wear their swords,
Long knives, at table. Forest, moor, and fen
Surround this hall that casts the only light,
This moment, in some nineteen miles of night.

Let's keep an eye on that one, Wulf, a true
Companion. Hair to shoulders, furrowed face
With little purplish blotches. Watch him chew
That sheep-leg, wiping mouth on sleeve, and chase
Each gobbet with a gulp of mead—a man
Immersed in *now*, in doing what he can.

His mouth is mostly open, to talk or eat
Or drink or laugh; not many teeth in there,
But lots of bread and mead and pulpy meat.
And that's what counts, he knows, that and his share
Of ruddy warmth with night-long tales, and old
Weapons, and heavy clothes, and reddish gold.

You see it in his lurching seaman-stride,
The way he lets his tankard bang on the board
As if to make a point; he's always tried
To act and be the way he could afford,
And in his strength and moods and wants, he's rich.
He fits his world as water fits a ditch.

You'd call him boastful. So would he, but he
Likes that, and shows it. Coming in he knocked
His snowy boots on the doorpost—like a tree
Smacked by an axe it rang, the timber rocked
A little. No one paid attention. Then
He swaggered shouting towards a gang of men

Hunched at table, and battered on the back
A man who shoved him hard with harsh guffaws
And hacking-gestures. Force enough to crack
A bone, but all in fun; till someone draws
His smaller knife and others draw away;
A word or move has maybe gone astray;

Looking through an "arrow slit" in
Bamburgh Castle on the Northumberland
coast, toward ruins on nearby Lindisfarne
Island (approximately five miles away). Both
sites, important in Anglo-Saxon times, are
here represented by later buildings.

But then he slices pork, not thane, and grins;
The others clash and spill their mugs, and toast
"May we be whole not holy!" Friendship wins,
Anger loses, for now. Then back to roast
Or sodden meat on slabs of barley-bread—
Half cooked or burned, half high or barely bled.

Everything here is made by hand or God.
They like things twisted—hilts and pitcher-handles,
Women's hair—as if to show the odd
Paths of perfection. Odors: tallow candles
Like burning bacon, wood-smoke twisting through
A single roof-hole, indoor barbecue

Of spitted sheep halfway from either end
(No fireplace, only flagstones, peat, and logs)—
An offering to a god with teeth, this blend
Of sizzling fat and resin, beasts and bogs
And woods. It kills the smell of men, but not
Of women; they have scents as highly wrought,

As rich, as any Grecian emperor's feast:
Perfumes of nearly mystical bouquet
Of wealth and spirit from the subtle east,
Unguents from silver jars that they display
As household jewels on chests along the wall.
It's always clear, this need to put it all—

Tapestries, goblets, horses, byrnies, rings,
Old swords, whatever's rich and beautiful—
Before the eyes of all. Yes, it's the things
They worship, not their market worth; like wool
Not judged by merchants but by freezing men.
For meaning is in things. But only when,

Like deer they've slain, the things are felt in turn
As something of the person, flesh of mind
And soul to body. No one could discern
A man per se, alone; a man's defined
By fathers, uncles, noted deeds, and all
Possessions, like the timbers of this hall

Warmed by those figured tapestries that stir,
Slightly, and set four feet in frozen earth,
In Denmark. Hrothgar, laced in otter-fur
And deerskin boots, amidst the food, is worth
What's visible, including thirty thanes;
He's faithful lord for life of what remains

When you deduct the ladies. All is lent;
And men and women equally preside,
Though men more often. Hrothgar's life is spent
Filling an order—everything implied
By *Hrothgar*. That takes lots of hunting, war,
Feasting, and gifts. But that's what life is for.

Wall planks from West Stow.

The fat-thick smoke has settled to their eyes,
Pork and bread to their stomachs. Mostly salt
For seasoning—and beer and wine, which rise,
Amaze the head, and leave a taste of malt
Or acid. Winter; little green to eat.
Enough of clove and pepper. Nothing sweet

But gold-rare combs of honey, heather-dark.
Each cuts a dripping hunk; they lick their hands.
The woods are full of meat. But here's no park
For private deer; Hrothgar ranges with bands
Of men and hounds, not foxhunt-gay but crude,
Relentless; not for sport, for heaps of food.

Sport too, but carcasses are all that count,
Finally, and let the final count be high!
Of deer, of boar; and let the falcons mount
The air, to kill the riches of the sky!
Food, sport, but dogged practice too, for when
They have the glory-hunt, the hunt of men.

For now the roast will do, turning in flame
And turned to charcoal outside, moist within.
The meal goes on; their moods and words grow tame;
The moment stretches out; they now begin
To look bemused, like men who understand,
At last, that what they have is time on hand,

A time that's free of calendars and clocks,
A bare, uncounted, unofficial now,
Densely immediate. With deepest shocks
From great events diffused as legend, how
Could history be a nightmare—or exist?
A nightmare's now, for any realist.

And these are realists of the everyday,
Fantasists of the night, whose nightmares lurk
Right there, outside the door. Or make their way
Up from the mere. "Right now" is time to work,
Or eat, or fight, or hear or tell a tale.
And measured, time's the drinking of this ale.

They look along the central ditch and fire:
Aescher stands at the end. Embraced in folds
Of greyish mantle is a light-brown lyre,
Size and shape of a tomcat, which he holds
The way you'd hold a cat. He strokes it lightly:
A sweet faint clang, reverberating slightly.

Ornamented stave church
door from Flaa, Norway.

"As Hrothgar built Hart without hands,
With a word the Almighty wrought our world,
This splendid land the sea surrounds;
And set triumphant sun and moon
As lights for men who live in the world.
First as a roof he raised up heaven,
Then made for men this middle-earth
Bespread with lovely limbs and leaves,
And gave at last life to all creatures,
To all that moves across the earth."

And more, in words of power locked in links
Like subtlest chain-mail, ringing in the air.
At pausing-points when Aescher deeply drinks,
All do the same; the table, hard and bare,
Rattles with heavy cups, like someone shaking
A rack of spears; the bard resumes his making.

Now fire and lights are low. The poem ceases
Not to applause but to a surge of talk
And clunk of cups, for poetry releases,
Like liquor, minds that hoard and tongues that lock
Our moods; but unlike liquor's, this release
Can cleanse the way of words, for poise and peace.

If you look inward, see, the doorway frames
The Danish view of heaven—hall-delight—
Now dying down. A servant smooths the flames
With scoops of ash, then bolts the door on night.
They bend to benches; king and queen have gone.
Wrapped in their cloaks, the men await the dawn.

"Keep from this hall, you of vague form,
Coiled on core of darkness, and warm
Only with blood from man and beast,
Moving up like fog to the feast:
By spears of barley that pierce the ground,
By shafts of the stream that lunges down,
By blades of light of the coming day,
All shadow-walkers keep away!"

Little it helped them, such a pagan charm.
For he was near, immense with strength, the one
Who walked in darkness meditating harm.
He couldn't bear that daily, when the sun
Went down, he heard from Hart the after-supper
Delights of harp and song. It made him suffer.

So they went on, the nights of winehall joy,
Until the alien one began to do
Unheard-of things, in order to destroy.
His name was Grendel. The wastes he wandered through,
By night, were fens; he left his giant spoor
Across the marshy fastness of the moor.

The sacrificial bog at the Archaeological
Research Center, Leire, Denmark.

23

He held the moors, his wind-flailed territory,
Grimly; for he was of the kin of Cain
Damned by God to repeat that ancient story
Of brother-killing. He was bound in pain
And rage, deformed, exiled forever far
From mankind, living where the monsters are.

The time had come. One night, when all the thanes
Had had their fill, he visited the hall;
He too was full—of hate and envy. The Danes
Were drunk, asleep. It wasn't a social call.
He pushed the great door wide and stood there, filling
The space and blocking moonlight. Merely killing

Was not enough: he savored meadhall-peace,
The sight of carefree Danes who'd just been fed.
At last, within a minute pain will cease!
These healthy, meaty bodies will be dead!
Enough. He closed his claws on one, who cried
Only a little. It was Wulf. He died

As boars are butchered, when the five-inch hooks
Ripped up his innards. No more mead for you,
Poor Wulf, or hunks of meat, or hungry looks
At servant-girls, or boasts of what you'll do
At sword-clash next; you have become the meat
That Grendel hangs on hooks to piecemeal eat.

Quickly he bent to others, slicing throats,
Gouging out guts, crunching the backs of necks
With teeth like steel; they died like pigs and goats
At Martinmas. He spattered walls with flecks
Of blood and flooded the floor, moving as fast
As swooping wolves, biting, slashing; at last,

Though he was silent as an eagle's wing,
The gasps and groans began to waken some
From drunken stupors; so in one last fling
He seized three more, awakened now but numb
Or paralyzed, and headed for his fen
Running for joy. He had killed thirty men.

Yes, it had been a lovely night, but not
For Hrothgar and his court. In reddening dawn
They saw writ large the price at which they'd bought
Their drunken feast. Now, after harp and song,
At Grendel's slaughter-skill they lifted high
In blood-bright Hart a mighty morning-cry.

Hrothgar, not boasting, sat amidst the mess.
He noted dully that the furniture
Was undisturbed, that benches suffer less
Than men—a truth that all the more seemed sure
As, faint, he watched the agonies of those
Not yet among the corpses laid in rows.

The monster image is adapted from an
illustration in *The Marvels of the East,*
bound up with the *Beowulf* manuscript.

Nor was it long, and not by invitation,
That Grendel came again. It would become
His custom, his expected recreation,
A need. He liked their flesh, and wanted some
Each day—bleeding or hung, fresh or decayed.
But thoughtful in his way, he never stayed

More time than necessary. Many Danes
Began to think festivities at Hart
Might be improved and life less fraught with strain
If things weren't quite so crowded. They would start
By sleeping elsewhere. So it was that all
Moved out to bowers, or further, and the hall,

Resplendent Hart, stood empty. Grendel's hate,
Like innocence, was pure; there was no way
To buy his friendship, or negotiate—
No one talks an eagle out of its prey.
Three winters had been dyed in Danish gore;
Each time, it seemed that they could take no more.

Like that of Hart and Hrothgar, Grendel's fame
Went through the world on verses: how a devil
That walked alone, a deadly shadow, came
To Hart by night to spread the realm of evil.
Where did he go? They didn't track his flight.
He held the misty moors in endless night.

If after weeks of respite drunken thanes
Slumped to sleep, forgetful, after the feast,
The monster came; he wouldn't leave his Danes.
Councils were useless. Then they thought, at least
There are the gods. And so at sacred well
And tree, as if to battle hell with hell,

They sacrificed in blood and called to Thor
And Tiw and others, wraiths who sniffed the smoke
Of burning chickens. That's what gods are for,
That and no more. So Hrothgar's spirit broke.
His hall disgraced, his company dispersed,
He had no hope—of all his pains, the worst.

But so intense was Grendel's hatred, long
And loathsome, that at last its fame arrived
Among the Geats. And one of them was strong;
So strong, no foe that fought with him survived
His giant grip. The monster from the fen
Interested him. And Hrothgar needed men.

He ordered that a vessel be prepared,
A good one; said he meant to see a king
Across the swan-road. No one gaped or stared
Or questioned; they assembled everything
He wanted; read the omens; wished him well.
Though he was dear, they knew what force compelled

The Oseberg ship.

27

The sudden moods of Higelac's young thane,
Moods that did not abate till turned to deeds.
Not even king and uncle could restrain
This prince, when he had wedded will to needs.
He picked as company the fourteen best,
The bravest he could find, whom he impressed

With both the danger and magnificence
Of their adventure; there would be no loot,
Only the hope of gifts and praise—and less
Of giving than of praising, which should suit,
He said, the hearts of heroes. He didn't plead,
For all were young; they instantly agreed.

He led to where the boat was, on the waves
Beneath a brooding cliff; the currents curled
Around the hull. As one whose energy craves
Release, the leader leaped aboard and hurled
His pack amidships; others did the same.
Men in the strength of youth are rarely tame.

However milky-dull the winter sun,
Their blades and byrnies shone like beacons—mail
Whose links a Weland-smith had one by one
Knit close together, swords that would not fail
If wielded well, all edged with welded strips
That shear through steel; the kind a hero grips.

With shouts and grunts the others shoved them off
And put the high-prowed wood-bound ship to sea.
Sped by a wind that screamed like eagles aloft
It sliced the ice-grey waters easily,
A foamy-throated swan through showers of hail
Scudding over the precincts of the whale.

The cold had bound their feet, its clamps of frost
Would not let go; behung with icicles
Their cloaks and beards partook of seas they crossed
And made them kin to icy-feathered gulls.
Night and snow from the north. They made their way
Far on the flood-ways till the second day.

They saw the sea-cliffs glitter in the distance;
Here were the steep and thick-set coastal hills,
Their goal. They felt a sudden snug resistance—
The prow bit sand. They'd passed the sea, which kills
And pays no wergild. Glad to be unhurt
They moored the boat, jingling in chainmail shirts

And thanking God. But on the cliff, unseen
By them, a guard was watching this procession
Along the gangplank; sunlight flashed on clean
And polished steel. As if to take possession
They came! Who were these men? He nearly broke
To know. He rode down, shook his spear, and spoke:

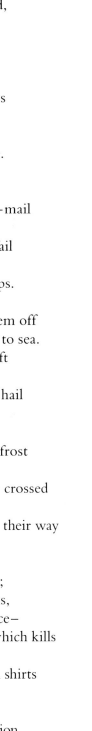

"What men are you? I guard this coast,
  Making sure that no ship-borne hosts
  Of marauders hit the Danes by stealth.
  I tell you, as to you yourselves
  I've never seen a crew of soldiers
  Approach more openly, or bolder—
  Although without our leave to land!
  And you: I've never seen a man
  Larger. Tell me your kin, your name,
  Lest you go forth among the Danes
  As spies. My thoughts come down to one—
  And answer fast!—where are you from?"

The leader answered: (He was big in fact,
  The tallest by a bit, but seemed not tall
  Because so wide—yet wiry and compact,
  Young oak condensed to man. His strength was all
  In massive arms, and chest four hand-spans large.
  A smile, a thick brown beard. He was in charge.)

"As to our people, we are Geats,
  Higelac's hearth-friends. As for me,
  My father Ecgtheow was a noble,
  A famous fighter, no one bolder.
  Old in winters he went his way;
  Those who know, remember his fame.
  Our purpose is benevolence.
  We've come to see your famous prince,
  The son of Healfdane, on an errand
  Of clear and great importance, bearing
  On what is known to all, I trust—
  But you must now enlighten us,
  And say if what I've heard is true:
  That some destroyer's hate pursues
  The Danes with slaughter after dark.
  If so, I've come to give you heart."

The mounted coastguard, fearless, spoke:
"A sharply thinking warrior knows
  How to judge works as well as words.
  Your words are fine; I've clearly heard
  Their good intent. So get your packs
  And shields and weapons—I'll go back
  To Hart with you, to show the way.
  Meanwhile I'll tell my men to take
  Your ship in hand, that fresh-tarred beauty,
  And guard it in a manner suiting
  Its worth, until you leave our shores.
  You will be still alive, I'm sure."

They left their broad-beamed ship and started out,
A twenty-minute march by beach and dune
And woods. No birds or flowers were about
Except for gulls. The frozen afternoon
Was closing down; their tread in the pinewood rang;
Their byrnies, bright with rings of iron, sang

In rhythm with their steps on ice-hard ground.
They were a jaunty troop that strode through cold
And growing dark, their gold-trimmed helmets crowned
By glittering effigies of boars—the bold
Protected by the wild. The leader thought
How good it was to see, before he fought,

The land as well as people he would save;
To fully taste the good that he was doing.
For grimly—unlike him who slashed a wave
With steel—he meant to win. Not by pursuing
Wraiths of splendor, but by getting his hands
On Grendel—to save these Danes, this hall, these lands.

The Hall appeared. The failing shafts of sun
Glanced from its gilded roof and made its walls
Seem dark, as if its life were nearly done.
For most, the site of horror-death appalls;
Here it was sad, the once-majestic head,
The hart's, appearing merely severed, dead.

Yes, this was Hart, the greatest hall on earth,
Hrothgar's; its light had lighted all the land.
The coastguard turned his horse and spoke these words
While pointing toward the Hall with a firm hand:

"You go ahead; I must go back
To guard the Danes against attacks
By sea. May God Almighty guard
You and your work till you depart!"

They passed unchallenged through the palisade,
Then rattled boards across the ditch, their sheer
Byrnies singing like chains; the noise they made
Aroused no sentry. Had the Danes no fear,
Or no more nerves? They took the stone-bright road
Right to the door; like conquerors they strode,

And no one noticed. Then a sullen clang—
They propped against the wall their shields and spears,
The grey tips pointing up. Their byrnies rang
Clear as they bent to benches. Had they ears,
These Danes?—The slow door groaned, as though in dread.
A man in rust-trimmed mail was there. He said:

"Who are you, with your gold-trimmed shields
And swords of serpent-welded steel?
You've come here, judging from your splendor,
Not in exile but for adventure."

The leader spoke: "Yes, we're not Danes
But Geats. Beowulf is my name.
We are Higelac's mead-companions.
I would like, if he would grant us
That wish, to speak with Healfdane's son,
Your famous lord. That's why I've come."

The herald Wulfgar (tall but thin
And bent and hollow-eyed, this prince
Of Wendels, old but not in years,
Renowned for wisdom far and near,
And valor) fixed his blinking eyes
On Beowulf and slowly replied:
"I shall, as you have asked, inform
Hrothgar the Dane that you have come
To see him. Then I'll bring the answer
Our mighty king sees fit to grant you."

He faded back inside the flickering dark.
In spite of fire the hall smelled dank, unused.
Dim in the shadows, bearing every mark
Of age though not yet sixty, slightly confused
At first by Wulfgar's hurry, Hrothgar sat
Drinking amidst the smoke of crisping fat.

Wulfgar, who knew the customs best
Of all, delivered an address
To Hrothgar seated with his thanes:
"From far across the hail-slashed main
Men of the Geats have come in suit;
They call their leader Beowulf.
They wish to speak, my lord, with you.
Gracious Hrothgar, do not refuse
Consent! These men are finely dressed;
One of them merits great respect."

The Viking Age hall
at Trelleborg, Denmark.

Interior of Trelleborg hall.

At last Lord Hrothgar raised his eyes
And spoke: "I knew him as a child.
His father's name was Ecgtheow, to whom
Hrethel the Geat had given home
His only child in marriage; now
The son has come here, seeking out
His family friend. Recall the gifts
We sent the Geats, that gold? Well if—
God grant it!—what our seamen said
Is true, we may be rescued yet:
They swore that this young fighting-man,
This prince of Geats, has in his hands
The strength of thirty men. I think
God has sent him against the fiend.
I'll give him treasure—yes, make plain
That they are welcome to the Danes!"
Wulfgar hurried, paused at the door,
And told the Geats, "My victory-lord,
The King of Danes, has bidden me
To say he knows your families
And that the men who've come so far
Are very welcome here at Hart.
Now you can go in battle-gear
To see the king; but leave your spears
And shields out there, till after council."
The strong one rose, his men around him;
A few remained—how all looked splendid!—
As weapon-guards. The others entered.

As Wulfgar led him under Hrothgar's roof,
The Geatish lord, before his eyes adjusted,
Smelled a decay, a moldy dampness, proof
Of need for cleansing; then he saw the rusted,
Ill-hung byrnies and helmets on the wall.
It struck him how indeed the mighty fall,

A phrase he'd heard but never quite believed.
Where were the armor-polishers, he thought.
He sensed that they had stopped as if relieved
Of duties by dishonor. Rust and rot,
Not shining pride, were proper now for Danes.
A corpse from which the color slowly drains,

That's what this hall is like, he thought with sadness
Cut by contempt: it savors of defeat,
Condition kin to grave disease and madness....
The fire played on the byrnie of the Geat
As if on silver fleece; his angled face
Focussed the drifting half-light of the place.

Posthole outline from
Leire Hall excavation.

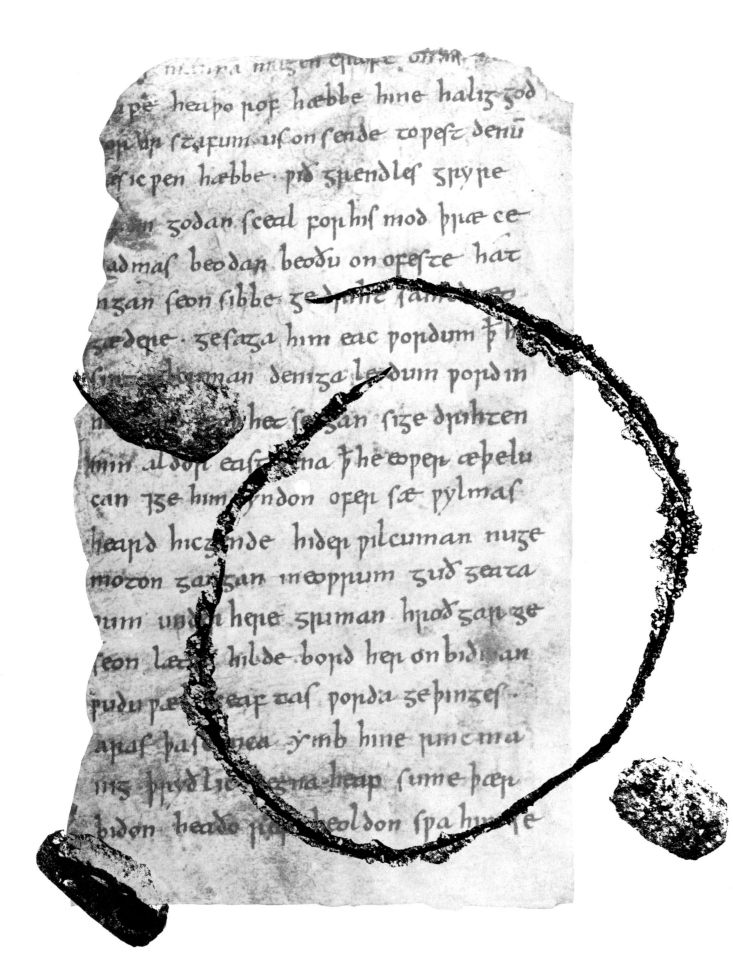

He stood at ease and set his gaze on one:
"Hrothgar, my lord, *wes hael!* I am the nephew
And thane of Higelac; you all know him,
And we of the Geats have heard of you and Grendel,
How Hart, the richest, proudest hall on earth,
Is after sundown empty as a skull,
Useless. Our seamen wished I'd seek you out;
They know my strength, they've witnessed what I've done:
The time I came all red from killing trolls,
Or wet from night-work on the waves, my victims
A dozen monsters from the deep I'd slain
With this short sword, which I have never used
Unless I've failed, somehow, to grip my foe;
It's safer, feeling fingers close on flesh,
More satisfying. Swords are second best.
I like destroying loathsome enemies,
I do it well. And so I wish to kill
Grendel, wish to grapple alone with him.
And now I beg you, brilliant lord of Danes,
Not to refuse, great prince, this single favor:
That I, with these good men, who've come so far,
Be given leave to cleanse your hall. I've learned
That Grendel scorns the use of sword and shield;
I will do likewise. We will leave to God
Which of us two will die by deadly hands.
I gather Grendel, given luck, would doubtless
Make of my carcass one more meal, a taste
Acquired from his dealings with the Danes.

We'll see. If he succeeds, two benefits
Ensue, my lord, to light your otherwise
Most dismal future: back to his fen he'd go,
Dropping my gore along the ground, partaking
Of me at home from time to time; you see,
No funeral costs if I'm digested food!
What's more, if I am food, no need to feed me.
Even the worst of fate dispenses favors.
But that's enough for now of pleasantries—
If Grendel slays me, send to Higelac
This best of battle-gear that guards my breast,
This ring-mail, Weland's work and Hrethel's heirloom.
Fate forever works the way it will."

His voice was deeply resonant but fine,
Weighting inflections as he slowly weighed
His choice of words. His discourse trod a line
Between the cultured and the brutal—staid,
But vibrant with a violence of will
Common in men whose pleasure is to kill.

...ða be beado... ...æt som...

secg wisode un der heorotes hrof...

under helme þ he on heoðe gestod beo

wulf maðelode on him byrne scan se

net seowed smiþes orþancum wæs þu hr

zar hal ic eom hige laces mæg ⁊ mago

ðegn hæbbe ic mærða fela ongunnen

on geogoþe me weayð spendles þing ea

minre eðel tyrf undyrne cuð secgað

sæliðend þ þæs sele stande reced sela[st]

rinca ge hwylcum idel ⁊ un nyt siððan

æfen leoht under heofenes haðor be

holen weorþeð þa me þ gelærdon leod

mine þa selestan snotere ceorlas þeo

den hroðzar þ ic þe sohte forþan hie

mægenes cræft mine cuþon selfe ofer

sawon ða ic of searwum cwom fah ⁊ from

feondum þær ic fife geband yðde eo

tena cyn ⁊ on yðum slog niceras

nihtes nearo þearfe dreah wræc

Silence prolonged the ending of his speech.
His Geatish accent lingered in their ears—
Outlandish, lilting—but what stayed with each,
Like fragrance, was a fading of their fears.
This warrior's will was not to be denied;
And he was Hrothgar's friend, and on their side.

Shadowed by heavy brows, and cheeks with bones
Both broad and slanting, just a little glint
Betrayed the eyes of Beowulf, their tones
Of palest grey and blue, and yet their print
Remained in eyes they met. He kept his stare
Steady on Hrothgar through the smoky air.

Hrothgar stayed in his seat, his long thin face
Raised to receive the stare; his beard-tip moved,
He spoke. The tenor voice was tense but firm:
"For deeds we've done, my dear friend Beowulf,
For favors done by friends you've sought us out.
I well recall the feud your father started,
When with his hands he killed poor Heatholaf
Among the Wylfings; then the Weder-Geats,
His people, fearing war refused him haven.
And so he turned to us, the Southern Danes,
Seeking across the waves the sons of Scyld.
I at the time had many treasure-towns,
Had just begun to rule in youth the realms
Of all the Danes (for Heregar had died,
My elder brother—he was better than I!),
So I prevented war, I sent the wergild,
Ancient gold, to the Wylfings over water;
And you have come to keep the oath he made.
I find it torture just to talk to you,
Or any man, of what he's done to me,
This Grendel, of his horrors wrought by hate.
Imagine coming to the hall one morning
And hearing not the clash of cups, and laughter,
And greetings, but the groans of dying men,
The threshing of their feet upon the floor—
Men you have loved!—and seeing the lucky ones,
The dead, all butchered, twisted, sprawled in blood.
Three years of this. These fighters have no fear
Of being wounded, killed in war, but here
No swords, no war—they die like pigs, except
Pigs are killed for a reason. Pointless fate
Has cut the numbers of my company,
Has swept my men into the maw of Grendel.
Ah, God could quickly end the senseless terror!
Not my fighters. Beer-drunk, often they boasted,
Still drinking, how they'd kill this devil-creature,
Wait and meet him with deadly steel in darkness;
And then as usual morning lit the mess,

The hall-gore, benches dripping with their blood.
But now, dear Beowulf, sit down to banquet.
It's time to hear of you; enough of troubles."

There was a scraping clunk of heavy wood
On wood as Hrothgar's men got up from table
To get more benches. Beowulf's men still stood
With hands on hips, by habit, to be able
To reach their knives instantly. Now, no need;
They started thinking of the crocks of mead.

The Geatish weapon-guards, invited in,
Came striding forth to smiles of welcome, hail
Of colleagues—heroes make a merry din
Drinking together! Jugs of mead and ale
Stood ready on the sideboards by the wall;
One of the thanes got big glass cups for all,

The kind with rounded base you can't set down
But have to hold till empty, then get more;
Another passed a pitcher foaming brown
With ale, then got a flask to brightly pour
The sheerest mead for Hrothgar and the Geats.
Time to think of victories, not defeats!

Beowulf watched the amber braid of mead
Flow from the damask-patterned silver flask,
Listened to clear-voiced Aescher; this indeed
Was joy! that Geats and Danes together bask
In ruddy warmth and light, and drink their fill,
Soon to be eating; nothing boded ill.

Then, sitting next to Hrothgar, Unferth spoke.
With sinews like heavy cord and bones like oak
He was a famous hero, fierce as flame,
But couldn't bear a rival to his name:
"You're large, friend Beowulf, but so's a cow.
Do you have other virtues? Tell us now,
Convincingly. It seems you like to swim.
Are you that Beowulf—a big lad, dim
Of wit—who with another imbecile,
Young Breca, risked his life with dauntless will
On winter seas, for no particular reason?
A swimming contest in the coldest season!
No one, not friend or foe, could hold you back.
You wallowed through the surging icy black
Plunging like porpoises. For seven nights
You measured sea-paths! Such are the delights
Of Norse and Geatish youth. And Breca won.
You were weaker, except as simpleton.
So if you dare to wait for Grendel, I fear
Prospects are not too bright for your career."

Beowulf sat impassive, merely staring
At Unferth. Then he smiled. "How very daring.
Your speech, my friend, displays a recklessness,
A genuine abandon; you care less
About your safety than one might expect.
Such folly is no different in effect
From courage. Call it courage. Though the beer
You swill by jugfuls tends to dull the fear
Someone like you would feel in speaking thus
To one like me. Your words are envious
And mostly false. So I'll recount the truth.
It's true that, in the glory of our youth,
Breca and I—and here you spoke with candor,
The only lapse to truth in your tale of slander—
Risked our lives in the churning winter sea.
He tried but couldn't draw away from me.
To deal with ocean brutes, we had in hand
Our naked swords; we drifted far from land
On welling waves whipped by a northern wind
In darkest night. The monsters, razor-finned
And sword-toothed, broke their blades against my mail,
My hard and hand-locked byrnie; shark and whale
And nicor came to grief upon my sword,
Were washed ashore. Now merchants could afford
To put to sea, the hazard less by much.
As to the contest: there's no threat from such
As Breca, not for me. No man is stronger
Swimming than I, can do it faster, longer.
When sunlight came I saw the Swedish coast
And got there first; I had made good my boast.
Fate often spares the man not doomed to die—
If he has strength and will. But Unferth, why
Have I not heard of your intrepid deeds?
Perhaps you keep them quiet? Yes, one needs
Discretion. Doubtless you were shy of fame
After you killed your brother—act of shame
For which you'll burn in hell despite your wit.
I tell you, were your strength and heart a bit
Consistent with your bragging, Unferth, it's clear
You victory-Danes would not be pale with fear.
I'll tell you what a Geat can do.
You've heard I have within these hands
The strength of thirty men.
But do you understand?
It means that with the effort you would need
To crush a pear that sweats with ripeness, I
Can grip a green hard apple big as a skull
And make its juice and pulp jet from between
My fingers. Strength and will are all.
My hands are large but not so much
Larger than yours; my will, to yours,
Is as a mallet to a willow-twig.

Which of you here can make his mind recall
All he has said today since waking? I
Can do that.
Or force his words to fit his very thoughts;
Or fingers absolutely to tighten?
You, in your realm of wishing, wanting,
Are in the twilight; I am in the sun,
Lens to his rays, focus of strength.
God is the sun, is light.
And so of course you've failed to stop
Grendel, you cannot wholly will to,
You cannot wholly think of Grendel.
But I, I think of Grendel, with a certain
Pleasure."

Hrothgar, hearing that word, began to smile;
And then he laughed—a louder, fuller laugh
Than Hart had heard these three hard years! And while,
In shock, the Danes sat back, he seized his staff,
Leaped up with cup in hand, cried to his men
"To Beowulf's pleasure! Drink!," then laughed again.

Then what a clash of cups and surge of laughter!
Shouts of "wes hael," toasts to the prince of Geats
Rang in the lofty hammer-beams and rafters!
They brought embroidered cushions for the seats,
Linen to drape the table, sprigs of pine
To grace the cloth, and wreaths of ivy-vine

To hang about the walls. Exquisite pain
For Grendel, were he listening outside,
Thinking his work had somehow been in vain!
Wealhtheow the queen came forth, in all her pride
Of gold-lit beauty, gravely smiling, pale.
Wisps of auburn strayed from beneath her veil;

Her graceful movement shaped at every fold
Her fine embroidered mantle, at her neck
Bound by a brooch of garnet-inlaid gold.
Her presence showed like ivy midst the wreck
Of winter. To the king she lifted up,
As if to consecrate, a golden cup

With rims of silver, surface densely chased
With twisted links and frets in floral design,
Rich as the pendant hanging to her waist.
She said, "be blithe, my lord, and drink this wine."
He nodded, took it, touched it to his lip.
She served each swordsman; each one took a sip.

o...ga beon hea dena ge hy...
pulſe ꝼolceſ hyꞃde þæt ꝼ...
ᵹe þoht dæt pæſ hæleþa hl...
hlyn ſpynſode, poꞃd pæꞃon pynſume
eode pealh þeoꝼ ꝼoꞃd, cpen hꞃoðᵹaꞃeſ
cyn na ᵹemyndiᵹ ᵹꞃette ᵹold hꞃo
den ᵹuman on healle þa ꝼꞃeolic
piꝼ ꝼul ᵹeſealde aꞃeſt eaſt dena
eþel peaꞃde bæd hine blidne æt þæꞃ
beoꞃ þeᵹe leodum leoꝼne he on luſt
ᵹe þeah ſymbel 7 ſele ꝼul ſiᵹe ꞃoꝼ
kyninᵹ ymb eode þa ideſ helminᵹa
duᵹu þe 7 ᵹeoᵹoþe dæl æᵹhpylcne
ſinc ꝼato ſealde, oþ þ ſæl alamp þæt
hio beopulꝼe, beaᵹ hꞃoðen cpen mode
ᵹe þunᵹen medo ꝼul æt bæꞃ · ᵹꞃette
ᵹeata leod ᵹode þancode piſ ꝼæſt
poꞃdum þæſ de hiꞃe ſe pilla ᵹelamp
þ heo on æniᵹne eoꞃl ᵹelyꝼde ꝼyꞃena
ꝼꞃoꝼꞃe he þ ꝼul ᵹe þeah pæl ꞃeop piᵹa

At last she gave the precious cup of wine
To Beowulf, and said with quiet voice:
"Dear friend, I thank our God that such a fine
Fighter has come; you would have been my choice,
If I had had to choose among them all.
My wish has happened. You will cleanse our hall."

Keeping his eyes on hers, the hero said:
"When I and my companions took to sea
I swore I'd save your Danes or end up dead
In Grendel's grip. I'll set this mead-hall free
Or do my best and die in here tonight."
At this the hall-folk saw the queen's delight

Spread in a lovely smile across her face.
She bowed slightly to Beowulf, then turned,
Glinting with beads and gold, and took her place
By Hrothgar. Though by now the roast was burned,
Carving the inner parts of pig released
Their juices for the sudden welcome-feast,

Soaking the dense-grained bread and veiling heads
Of hungry men with swirls of fragrant steam.
At last they talked and ate in joy, instead
Of fear. But soon, as if to break the dream,
Hrothgar stood up, prepared to seek his rest,
To end the little feast. He was oppressed

By knowledge that the devil-thane since dawn
Would have been planning death for many Danes
As soon as shadow-shapes of night came on.
Everyone rose. Like someone who explains,
Hrothgar addressed the Geat: "never before,
Since I've been king—nor will I ever more—

Have I entrusted Hart to anyone.
Now have and hold this best of houses! Wake
Against the wrath to come, so that the sun
Will see your triumph. If, for God's own sake,
You win, I'll give whatever gifts you want."
He slowly left, kingly but bent and gaunt,

And with him went the Danes. The Geats prepared.
A slave brought mattresses with feather-beds
And pillows for the benches. No one dared
To strip off armor, leaving throats and heads
And bodies free, and no one could have slept,
Or tried to sleep, without his sword...except

geþeod · ⁊ þ rond acþæð · Næfre ic ænegu[m]

men æt alyfde siþðan ic hond ⁊ rond heo

ban mihte ðryþ ærn dena buton þe nuða

hafa nu ⁊ ge heald husa selest ge myne

mærþo mægen ellen cyð waca wið wraþum

ne bið þe wilna gad gif þu þis ellen weorc aldre

· x ·   · ⁊ ge dige[st]

 A him hroþ gar gewat mid his hæ

leþa ge dryht eodur scyldinga ut

of healle wolde wig fruma wealh þeo we

can cwen to ge beddan hæfde kyning

wuldor gewealde to geanes sweg umen

ge frungon sele weard asette sund or nyt

te be heold ymb aldor dena eoton weard

abead hwi wi gearwa leod geong ne cwi wode

modgan mægnes metodes hyldo · ða hebi

op dyde isern byrnan helm of hafe lan

sealde his hyrsted sweord yrena cyst om

biht þegne ⁊ ge heald ðan het hilde geatwe

ge swæc hæfe goda gylp worda sum · beowulf

Beowulf. Shunning war gear—byrnie, sword,
And helm—he gave it to a thane to keep.
His men were stunned. He said, "I can afford
To go unarmed; and victory would be cheap
With sword and mail, which Grendel doesn't use.
I'm no weaker in war than he. I choose,

Then, to meet him on equal terms. And you,
My friends: don't interfere! Let God decide."
He lay on his back, uncovered, and in view—
Perfectly—from the door. The one who died,
Hondscio, lay in the darkness near the door,
Staring, thinking of Geatland. Nevermore.

It came. The shape of the shadow-strider
Moved toward Hart from the frozen moors
Through snow that hissed at him like snakes,
Darkly; clouds had covered the moon.
The fighter-guardians dozed in fear,
All but one of them; he, awake,
Waited in growing rage for Grendel.

Grendel, the cursed of God, was coming;
Up from the fens through falling snow,
Meditating murder at Hart.
At last he saw the mead-hall looming
White in the moon; the clouds had moved,
The snow like smoke swirled from the roof,
Whipped by a bitter wind. So pure,
It seemed. He paused to gloat on the scene,
Thinking how screams would blast the silence,
How blood would soon be fouling snow.
He knew, from many nights at Hart,
What to expect; but a surprise
Was waiting, a different kind of welcome.

He had come to the Hall—the killer,
God-cursed giant bereft of joy.
He gripped and bent the boar-head handle,
Jerking the door, disjointing it—
Though fire-hardened, iron failed;
It hung ajar, a broken jaw.
All was sudden, such was his rage;
Unlovely fire that lit his eyes
Flared as he saw the stretched-out men
He meant to kill. The Geat was quiet,
Trying to wait until his victim
Was well inside the hall. So swift,
Then, was the devil, that a horror
Happened before the prince could help:
Thrusting talons into the throat
Of Hondscio, biting through the bonelocks
That bound his shoulder, arm, and breastbone,
Grendel drank from the gaping veins
And gorged on huge gobbets of flesh.

Interior of the hall at Trelleborg.

48

Then, in a single stride, extending
One arm, he bent to Beowulf.
Before the talons touched his body
Beowulf rose, braced by his elbow,
And took the hand the fiend extended.
The monster knew, that very moment—
No doubt was possible—that death,
And not the death of a Geat, was near.
He'd never met, had not imagined,
A grip like that. His fear was great,

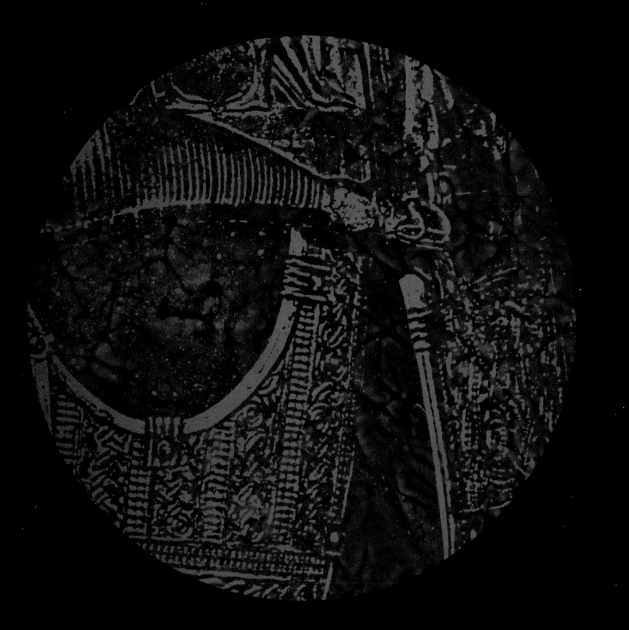

His only wish to get away.
Beowulf got to his feet; he grasped
The hand so firmly, fingers burst
And spurted blood through splintered bones.
This devil killed but didn't fight;
The hero wanted him at Hart,
To give him final Geatish welcome.
Their disagreement caused a din.
It was a wonder how the wine-hall,
However strong, withstood that grappling:

Many a bench though bound with iron
Lost with a rending crack its legs,
The twelve-foot table overturned,
Chests with crockery clashed with floorboards,
The walls shook with the sudden shocks–
Danes had thought it couldn't be damaged,
Unless it were rapt by flames at last.
But worst of sounds was Grendel's wail,
A high-pitched slaughter-scream that pierced
The Danes who trembled far in terror,
Gathered close by the ditch together.
The Geatish prince, grimly at work,
Was silent. His men, in spite of orders,
Had started flailing fecklessly
At Grendel with swords and spears and axes,
Seeking the monster's soul with steel.
Their arms were weak as if bewitched;
Their blades, like parchment, wouldn't bite;
Grendel ignored them, grappling with death,
With Beowulf. The hero wanted,
Without delay, to take his life,
However little that life was worth.
No chance for Grendel to get away;
Beowulf had him by the hand.
Each of them loathed the other living.
Then Beowulf, with both his hands,
Bending the arm behind its back
Jerked it upward, ripping the joint.
With sounds of rending, sinews tore–
The heavy bonelocks burst at last.
Disjointed like a chicken, joyless,
Lighter by an arm, the lone one,
Free at last, ran for his fen,
Trailing streamers of blood and screams.

Beowulf had made good his boast.
The prince laughed loud in pride of night-work,
Received the joy of his men with joy.
Then as a sign for all to see
He climbed the roof with Grendel's claw,
The shattered limb, shoulder and all,
And hung it on the antlers of Hart
Both high and clear. The Hall was cleansed.

As morning cut the shadows, bathing snow
On the roof in lukewarm light and turning ice
That hung in spears from the eaves to drops, first slow,
Then rapid, fighters who had feared the price
And ceased to visit, started to arrive
To see the sign that Hart had come alive:

Grendel's grip, with its vicious claws all curled
And, stiffly angled, rended shoulder and arm
Caught in the antlers, showing to the world
That he was dead. To see that grisly charm,
Pledge of safety, princes from everywhere
Were coming in, to stand and talk and stare.

Then all together took a cautious ride
Along the trail of bloody melting snow
Until they came to where the monster died,
His mere; the body must be there below—
The trail had stopped at the reddish reeds and mud
Where water was a swirl of icy blood.

Here hell had claimed the lone and joyless one.
Riding back the warriors raced their horses,
Medley of stallions dappled, bay, and dun,
Leaping bushes, finding such racing-courses
As snowy meadows offered, making cheer
By shouting bets of cups for mead and beer

And singing of Beowulf's relentless grip
(Nor did they fail to mention Hrothgar the good).
Morning broadened; horses continued to slip
And splatter in the mud; now Hrothgar stood
With Wealhtheow on the steps of Hart, amazed
At how the feud had ended. Long they gazed,

Caught by the glinting roof and Grendel's hand.
Beowulf left the hall where he'd been sitting,
Telling the Spear-Danes how it all had happened,
And greeted Hrothgar, glad at last, and Wealhtheow.
The Danish lord then looked at Beowulf,
Gesturing at the gable: "God be thanked,
And soon, for such a sight! The arms and claws
Of Grendel have never given me such pleasure.
In truth, that lady—if she's still alive—
Who brought forth Beowulf can say that God
Gave her his fullest grace in childbirth. Now,
Beowulf, best of men, I mean to take
You as my son, to love you as my life;
Hold to your new connection, now and always!
You'll never lack for wealth of the world I wield.
Often I've given gold to tamer fighters,

For lesser deeds. But you have done such things,
Your name will last for ever. Now may God
Bless you and grant you, all your life, his gifts!"

Beowulf answered, "what a feat it was,
Killing that devil–I wish you'd seen him die!
I thought to make his deathbed, lay him down
For good and break his neckbones in my grip,
But God had other thoughts and let him go.
I failed, I couldn't keep the fiend from leaving;
He was too good at fleeing from a fight.
But as a souvenir, to save his life
He left his hand behind–and arm, and shoulder.
Not the cleverest way to keep alive.
He's dead at home, awaiting there God's doom."

Everyone marked how quiet Unferth was,
How disinclined to brag of battle-deeds,
Now that the men could see the arm and claws
That Beowulf had fixed to the Hall, which bleeds
Now with the blood of Grendel, not their own–
The five-inch steely claws that sliced through bone!

This time he'd hurt the Hall far more than men,
All but one of them. Hrothgar's people cleaned
And fixed the damage, making Hart again
What it had been before the stinking fiend
Had made it his latrine and slaughter-shed
(Often, as if to claim it, as he fled

He dropped his dung along the floor, its stench
Worse than a hundred rotting hogs in summer).
Picking up splinters, joining leg to bench,
Replacing bolt and hinge, noting the number
Of vases, crocks, and cups to make or buy
But mostly scrubbing wood with watered lye,

Burning resin, or hanging sweet dry heather
From rafters–all pursued a single goal,
To clean all trace of Grendel now, forever,
From shattered Hart, its roof alone still whole,
Spared by Grendel's lunging for life and breath.
In vain: he's stretched upon the bed of death.

Now men and women took the tapestries
From bronze-locked chests of oak to hang on walls:
In one, a clearing where the bloodhounds seize
A plunging boar; and then the quarry falls
Pierced with a golden spear (for everywhere
Is woven gold–the hunters' cloaks and hair,

The sun and autumn leaves); in others war,
The flash of sword at flesh, brightens the hall
With gold and scarlet dripping roof to floor,
With blades and blood, till every foot of wall
Is covered. Cushions of red-embroidered silk
On benches, linen creamy white as milk

On tables, twists of ivy to mark each place,
And banners hanging from the hammer-beams
Like tongues of fire: brilliant cloth with lace
Or braid or interlacing flower-schemes
Everywhere hid the dark of wood, the dark
Of Grendel. He had made his heavy mark;

The Danes obscured it with a blazing feast.
Amidst the flame-lit hues and clinking cups
Hrothgar entered. The random laughter ceased;
From liquor-tempered throats a cheer went up
That rang in the roof, they clashed their hands so hard
Table-candles went out and flames of tarred

Torches in sconces on the wall were bent!
Hrothgar bowed a little, his wavy hair
Of shoulder length fell forward to a tent
That hid his smile. His mantle trimmed with vair,
Closed with a silver clasp, his tunic dense
With woven gold and gems, buckle immense—

A three-pound mass of interlacing gold—
Hrothgar presided. Danes were drunk already.
You notice those just entered from the cold:
When going for the mead, their stride is steady.
I've never heard of greater hall-joy, men
Immersed in drinking. Even Hrothulf, then,

Drank with his uncle. All today were friends;
No traitors.—Hrothgar raised a steady hand;
The riot lessened, as a calm descends
Slowly on tossing trees. At his command
The nailed-oak door, restored to strength, swung wide;
The leader beckoned Beowulf to his side

As four men bearing gifts came through the door.
Each halted in his turn before the Dane,
Who passed the gifts—no man had seen such four
Glittering treasures!—slowly from his thane
To Beowulf, and toasted him who'd freed
Their Hall. Four times they drained their cups of mead,

Four times the hero lifted up a prize
For all to see: a gilded silken banner,
Helmet with brows of steel to guard the eyes,
Supple byrnie, and, finest work of hammer
And file, a sword with serpent-pattern, made
By beating silver chains into the blade.

Then Hrothgar gestured toward the door again,
And what a clatter!—eight large horses led
Right up to Beowulf, fine as the men
Who led them. All had gold about the head,
And one was saddled with the battle-seat,
Bejewelled, of Hrothgar. All was for the Geat—

Horses, treasure—to pay him for his fight;
This was no stingy lord! He bade his guest
Enjoy the gifts; all could see the delight
Of Beowulf. Then Hrothgar thanked the rest,
Beowulf's men, and gave them ancient swords
And paid, for Hondscio, gold, and gracious words.

(How many more the monster would have killed
Had not the Lord protected them from fate,
The Lord and Beowulf the iron-willed!
Those who live for long in this warring state,
The world, know much of evil, much of good.)
But now to eating. Hart, which had withstood

The shock of Grendel, shook anew to shocks
Of joy, as Hrothgar blessed and broke the bread,
Men thumped applause on boards, and slaves with crocks
Of heated water made the rounds and spread
Towels before the guests; then swirls of steam
Mixed with the hall-smoke—soup of leeks and cream,

First course, had come; then quickly more, the slaves
Bending with platters on their shoulders, rushing,
Bumping each other, passing food on trays,
Sloshing mead and beer on the floor and crushing
Fruit underfoot. They brought roast pork with cloves
And saffron, dying trenchers cut from loaves

Of feastday white; and pots of lentils packed
With carrots, onions, chunks of chicken, ham,
And garlic; smoking pheasants; shellfish cracked
And gaping—even women worked to cram
Their stomachs with abundance. No relief
All day, all night. When Hrothgar's favorite, beef

Fresh killed and roasted till the surface charred,
Came in the form of cow- and ox-joints whole,
After the geese and ducks preserved in lard,
Each man was but a mouth, his heart and soul
Were in his stomach. Those who'd gorged on game,
Venison salted, smoked, or broiled, felt shame

To fail the challenge of beef. There was no space
For all the silver dishes on the linen. . . .
Hrothgar asked that Beowulf take a place
Beside him, as his son; the noble women,
His wife and daughter, many times got up
And went around to hand the studded cup,

Its ancient gold flowing with tawny mead,
To Geats and favored thanes, with words of cheer
From Wealhtheow to them all (they didn't need
An invitation to the meat and beer)—
Wealhtheow, splendid in spiral arm-rings, walking
Throughout the hall, and Freawaru talking,

Demurely, to a few; she was betrothed
To Ingeld, prince of Heathobards. By now
Night pressed, but no more fear: the one they loathed,
Wearied by wounds, had fared on the forth-way, bowed
To darkness.—Hrothgar touched the harpstrings. Old
In deeds, remembering much, he slowly told

His tales of wonder, woe, and truth,
Of Danes he'd known, their strength in dying.
Then Hrothgar passed the harp to Aescher
The favorite, asked to hear of Finn,
Of Frisian slaughter. Aescher struck
The gleewood loudly, then began:

"After the Danes had settled down
At Finnsburg, peaceful with the Frisians
So Hnaef could visit Hildeburh,
Brother could see his royal sister
Who by her wedding wove the peace—
One night half-way to dawn the watch,
Keen at the doorway, cried to Hnaef
He'd seen a light of sun or fire;
But Hnaef the king could see more clearly:
'No, it's not dawn or dragon-fire,
It's moonlight striking steel—awake!
They're coming for us! Now the cry
Of eagles will be heard, and wolves,
Feeding after the fight on flesh,
After the shields and shafts have met—
Get up! Look to your mail, your linden,
Take up your swords and spears, take courage!'
They did; they formed around the door,
Sigeferth foremost, prince of Sedgans. . . ."

Aescher took breath and drink; the others drank,
The ladies passing goblets. He went on,
How sixty thanes knew how to kill to thank
Their leader Hnaef for mead, and how at dawn
All still were standing, and for five dawns more
The Danes cut down the Frisians by the door. . . .

"After the final night of fighting,
Both sides not weak in will but numbers—
Byrnies had sounded terror-songs
All day, and bows had briskly hummed—
By morning's grey the mourning lady,
Hildeburh, son and brother slain,
Saw through her tears the slaughter-field

And all her pride and pleasure gone.
The little remnant, byrnies rent,
Breathing with pain and bleeding hard,
Helpless to further harm each other,
Halted and parleyed, Finn with Hengest.
The terms that Hengest tendered were these:
The Danes would have a private hall,
And they would share and share alike,
Daily, with Frisians–Finn would give
As richly of gold-thick rings to them
As to his own. The oaths were taken.
Finn pledged his men would never mention,
Either, by way of scorn or envy,
How Danes were forced to follow the killer
Of Hnaef their lord; if someone laughed,
The slip would be repaired by sword-edge.

"They built a pyre for all the bodies,
First laying many loads of straw,
Then tinder-sticks, then fresh-cut timber
Of oak and beech and ash and birch
Scattered with resin, spices, flowers–
Twenty feet high, a hundred long.
Many a blood-dark byrnie there,
And brightly gilded boar's-head helmets
Laid with the heroes who had worn them.
Hildeburh said to place her son
Beside his uncle. Then she sang,
Hair down, the saddest song of all
As Danes and Frisians set the fire.
The mourners cast their cloaks and shields,
Mugfuls of wine and milk and blood
Into the fire, which roared as fiercely
As stormy surf and wound to the sky
In fat-black spirals. Skulls were melted,
Blood from the heated corpses burst
From gash-wounds. Fire, the greedy spirit,
Swallowed the best of both the nations.

"Frisians went back to farms and fishing,
But Hengest stayed behind with Finn,
A winter slaughter-stained for Hengest
Thinking of how his thanes had died.
Brooding on home was likewise hopeless;
The North Sea locked them in for now
With steely ice and night-dark storms
That brought the deep to coldest boil.
But seasons hurry, spring arrives
With wonder-brilliant weather, ending
Winter death as it always does,
So Hengest thought again of home–
But even more he yearned for murder,
Sacred revenge, the sweetest killing.
He spent the long days planning, swearing
His fingers would remember Finn

With iron; mentally he marked
The place, along the pale soft neck.

"Hengest didn't refuse his duty
When cold with hate Hunlafing came
And knelt and laid across his knees
Burnished, gigantic "Battleflame,"
Its edges famed among the Frisians,
Finest of swords. Yes, Finn would suffer
The sudden, all-destroying vengeance
Of Danes for kinfolk killed, at night—
But not as Hengest hoped and planned.
Even too quick for him it came:
One night at drinking, two rough Danes,
Guthlaf and Oslaf, saw a grin
They thought a Frisian flicked at them.
Instantly Guthlaf gutted the man
And Oslaf nailed another's hand
To the table, Danes with death in mind
And swords in hand surged at the Frisians...

"...And so the floor was slick with blood
And Finn was killed, the king amidst
His men, and Danes took down to their ship
The queen and all that they could carry
Of Finn's possessions—fighting-gear
And jewels, golden goblets, platters—
And sailed away. That splendid woman
Went back to Denmark, with her Danes."

After a hush, applause broke forth, and shouts
And laughter; Aescher's high-domed head went back,
He raised his wine-cup; Wealhtheow went about,
Bright with her hair and crown against the black
Of shadows, serving Hrothgar still at one
With Hrothulf sitting there, his brother's son;

And Unferth too was there at Hrothgar's feet,
Praised for his courage though with sword he'd murdered
His brother. Wealhtheow bent to her husband's seat:

"Receive this cup, my king, dear Hrothgar, ring-lord!
Be glad, and be as generous to the Geats
In gifts as in your words, for that is good.
Enjoy your riches while you reign, and leave
Our well-loved sons your kingdom when you die.
I know my gracious Hrothulf here—dear nephew!
I know if you, my lord, must leave the world
Before him, Hrothulf will with honor wield
Your power, rule your people for our children;
Especially, I know he'll pay our sons
The goodness we showed him, if he remembers
All that we did for him when he was little,
All for his pleasure and profit that we did."
She went to the bench where both her sons were sitting,

Hrethric and Hrothmund, with the men of Hrothgar
As well as Beowulf the good, the hero.

They brought the cup to Beowulf. He took
Their wine and friendship and another round
Of gifts as well: Hrothgar raised up and shook
A gold-chased byrnie—such a gentle sound
Of jingling mingled with darting glints of fire!—
And brought forth rings of twisted golden wire;

But best was one great neckpiece, gems and gold—
The best since Hama stole the Brosings' necklace
From Ermenrich the vicious. More than bold,
Hama, in braving Ermenrich, was reckless
But lived and bore his treasures to the Tower,
The bright one. Beowulf's neckpiece, grown in power,

Went to Higelac later; in his pride
He wore it when he raided Friesland, asking
For trouble; there beneath his shield he died.
The place reserved for corpses, when the axing
Had stopped, was held by Geats.—With cheers the men
Approved these gifts. Then Wealhtheow spoke again:

"Enjoy, dear Beowulf, this jewelled necklace
And Hrothgar's byrnie. Be a good adviser
To these young men and I'll remember that
With fine rewards! Your fame, for what you've done,
Has crossed the wind-yard, far as the waves are blown.
Prosper while yet you live, my happy prince!
And specially be kind to these my sons.
But all is well here; every thane is true
To every other, loyal to lord and lady,
And, as you see, in perfect peace. These thanes,
All drunk—good fellows all!—do as I bid."

She took her seat, smiling a puzzling smile.
Deep was the night, the tables had been cleared,
The drinking stretched on merrily a while,
Of choicest mead; forgetting all they'd feared,
Forgetting fate, the Scyldings as before
Stayed in the Hall. One settled near the door,

Which he should not have done. When Hrothgar left
They brought out cushions, blankets, mats to spread
On benches. Each, by cautious habit, slept
With helmet and spear at side and shield at head.
They didn't care to be surprised, for then
They couldn't help their lord. They were good men.

hrægles neot þeo ge streona

tela cen þec mid cræfte ⁊ þyssum cny

wes lara liðe ic þe þæs leange man ha

þu ge fered þ ðe feor ⁊ neah ealne wide

weras ehtigað efne swa side swa sǽ be

wind geard weallas wes þenden þu lifige æ

eadig ic þe an tela sinc gestreona beo þu

suna minū dædum gedefe dream heal

de her is æghwylc eorl oþrum ge trywe

modes milde man drihtne hol þegnas sy

don ge þwære þeod eal gearo druncne dr

guman doð swa ic bidde. Eode þa to setle

þær wæs symbla cyst druncon win weras wy

ne cuþon geo sceaft grimme swa hit agan

gen wearð eorla manegū syþðan æfen cwom

⁊ him hroþgar ge wat to hofe sinum rice

to ræste reced weardode unrim eorla swa

hie oft ær dydon benc þelu beredon hit

geond bræded wearð beddum ⁊ bolstrum

beor scealca sum fus ⁊ fæge flet ræste ge

They sank to sleep, a sleep from which the one
At rest beside the door would not return.
One simple truth–that Grendel's life was done–
Lulled them to sleep; but they were soon to learn,
Swiftly and unforgettably, another
Less soothing truth: that Grendel had a mother

Who could avenge her son. Long had they lived
In hideous love together, where the stream
Fell coldly on the slopes, brooding amid
The water-terrors in their endless dream
Of hell, the heirs and kin by blood of Cain
Whose crime had marked them with a scarlet stain.

Grendel had found his executioner;
But in that dim denatured woman, large
And lithe, intent on misery, in her
Who'd borne him, he had one who could discharge
His debt of hate–perfect avenger. Grieving,
Silent, she took the path of Grendel, leaving

Big prints and screeching squirrels and a stench
To mark her passage. Wrapped in night alone
She came, leaping the planks across the trench
For silence. Like a cat that chews a bone,
Intense, eyes shut then looking up, she'd chewed
Her hate and hurt till nothing could intrude.

Hart was abuzz with snores of drunken Danes.
The Geats were elsewhere. All was peaceful. Then
A stinking sweetness that had touched the brains
Of several, woke them, just as two more men,
Whose dreams were bad, observing that the door
Was open, felt the chill of something more

Than winter. . . . like a house of straw, their peace
Went with the wind: one yelled, then others, then
Fumbling, lunging in darkness, screams increase,
Torches lit from embers, crashing again,
All grabbing for their swords and shields–no time
For helms and byrnies! For the terror-crime,

The slaughter-dark was back, with female force–
Less than male as she-wolf's is less than bear's
But quicker, sharper, from a boundless source
Of single-minded hatred. At the flares
Of fire and shouts and clatter she took fright
But also, fleeing swiftly toward the night,

She took in a sudden swoop the man who'd stayed
Beside the doorway, slipping with her hooks,
Him twisting, so his back was well-nigh flayed,
A man of lovely voice and gentle looks,
Hrothgar's favorite. And even though pursued,
She took down Grendel's hand. And so the feud,

Creatures from *The Marvels of the East*
framed by a silhouette of the manuscript. In
the background is an enlarged passage of
the *Beowulf* manuscript describing the
coming of Grendel's mother, named in the
bottom line.

At greatest cost to either side, went on. –
Just as they sent for Beowulf, the door
Opened to him, arriving with the dawn
And all his men. They strode across the floor;
The hallwood dinned. Their beaming prince went right
To Hrothgar, asked if he'd had a restful night.

"Don't ask about my 'restful night,' so brightly!
Dead is Aescher my evening minstrel–dead,
He who had been my shoulder-friend in battle
When sword on boar-helm crashed, each keeping watch
Over the other; quick to think at counsel,
Brilliant with words and tales as with a sword,
Yrmenlaf's elder brother, my bard, my friend,
Is dead! The wandering devil-spirit took him,
Bringing fear and grief again to the Danes.
Yes, she has made it more than even now,
As all my men agree: they mourn for Aescher,
Selfless giver of good. His hand is stilled."
The king fell silent for a minute, staring
Emptily; Hart was silent. He resumed:
"I've heard my people–farmers, hall-thanes–say
They've seen at twilight two such alien creatures,
Giants, walking the wasteland of the moors;
They half discerned that one was woman-shaped,
The other like a man but far more mighty.
Time out of mind they've called this monster Grendel,
Kinless but for the female. In the fens
Is where they live, among the misty trails–
The secret land, wolf slopes and windy headlands
Where winding streams fall on the darkened stones.
Not far from us–in miles–is Grendel's mere,
Shrouded with frost-encrusted shrubs, and groves
Of heavy-rooted trees that overhang it.
There on warm nights you see, across the surface,
The fearsome marvel of running, darting fire;
And none has ever known what's on the bottom
Or touched it. Stags, they say, pursued by hounds,
Would sooner die on shore than save their lives
By plunging into that uncanny pool!
From it, dim vapors coil up to the clouds;
Winds come, the air turns black, the heavens weep....
We need your help again. I'm not at ease
In asking you to go to Grendel's hall,
That deadly sinkhole. Seek it if you dare!
I'll give you ancient treasure, twisted gold,
Just as before, as fee if you survive."

Beowulf spoke: "No fear, wise prince! It's better
To take revenge than mourn a friend too much.
We all must die. But those with force will do,
Before their death, such deeds as live in glory.
Then up, my wine-friend! We must go and track,
Quickly, the Grendel-creature. This I promise:
No matter where she flees–the thickest forest,

The deepest cave, the quiet ocean floor—
She won't escape. Take comfort, then, from me."
Hrothgar arose, praised God for what he'd heard.

Then Hrothgar's splendid horse, of moonlight hue
And braided mane, was bridled and led up;
Beowulf was superbly mounted too;
The men would walk. Once more they passed the cup,
Whetting their mood with fire, and started off.
Easy tracking: the half-thawed ground was soft,

They saw the splayed-out footprints far ahead
Along the forest paths, across the moor,
Driven yet deeper in the ground by dead
Weight from the ripped and dripping corpse of poor
Beloved Aescher. Then the twisting climb
Through brambled paths, on ledges slick with slime

Till Hrothgar, scouting with the vanguard, stopped,
Raising his light-gloved hand. He pointed down
To where the tree-line sloped away then dropped
Suddenly; through the mesh of trees around
They saw a pool as dead and grey as stone.
All stood together; each man felt alone.

Below this cheerless wood, some water turned
In slow and bloody swirls.—And Hrothgar wailed
With rage and grief, the eyes of Danes all burned
In tears, when at the shore they found, impaled
High on a stake, the head of Aescher, face
In shreds, exposed to ravens, to disgrace.

As with repeated clanging notes the horn
Called to assembly on the shore, a sound
Of muted splashes in response was borne
Slowly through stagnant air; they looked around
And saw pale slug-like creatures drop from rocks,
The water barely rippling at the shocks.

A Dane took aim at one: the arrow passed
All the way through and shattered on the stone,
Another with his spear had hooked it fast,
They hauled it in. It seemed to have no bone,
No face. Except for one, all stood amazed;
Except for Beowulf, they stood and gazed.

He was intent on work, on putting on
His armor: first the byrnie, knit with rings
Hard as diamond but light as finest lawn,
And then a helmet where the sword-edge sings
But cannot bite, forged by a smith long dead
Who carved along its crest a great boar's head.

Olaus Wurmius's prospect of Gamle Leire
(1643), taking us into the Danish geography
of the poem. His capital letters designate
antiquities at this site, long thought to be the
seat of the Scylding kings of Denmark. Here
Hrothgar might have built his hall.

Then Unferth, strong in boldness, who'd forgot
What he had said when ugly-drunk, came up
To lend the Geat his sword, called Hrunting, wrought
So sharp that, held in water, it could cut
A sheep-size tuft of wool the current brought it
As swift and smoothly as it cut the water.

Hardened in battle-blood, with twig-like patterns,
Hrunting had failed no hero handling it.
But not for Unferth now; he knew his better.
Beowulf spoke: "remember what we said,
Son of Healfdane, now that I'm set again
To risk my life, to die for you and the Danes:
That if indeed I die, you'll be a father
To me your vanished son, and to my men
A strong protector; that you'll send my treasures,
Dear Hrothgar—those you gave—to Higelac,
So when the Geat-lord gazes on that wealth
He'll know I'd found a good and mighty gold-friend.
And give my wave-marked sword to worthy Unferth;
Hrunting will get me glory. Or death will take me."

Not waiting for reply, he walked
Slowly to where a dead limb stretched
Above the pool. He paused a moment
Then waded in. The water took him,
Closing upon him quietly.
Faintly he hears the shouts of friends
Through a breathtaking blur of water,
Dimmer the further down he swims,
The chill embracing every bone,
Quickly fastening them with clamps;
Silence is total now, the stillness
Dreamlike, his sense of up and down
Going, but still he seeks, himself
The handsome bait to bring her forth....

Far in the depths, the creature feels
A sudden shock: something has entered
The upper reaches of her realm,
Alien, and coming ever closer.
Adept in every darkness, hate-strong,
Like a harpoon she flies to him
And takes his arm with greedy talons,
Would have mauled him but for his mail;
She leads him downward eagerly
And draws him through a sudden den-hole,
Out of the black of binding water;
Daunting firelight dazzles his eyes;
Just as he glimpses, glazed with fire,
Her crudely female form beside him—
Pale hide, thick clots of hair, immense—
Already she has come around him,
Is trying powerfully to trip him;
Still water-numb, all but his will,

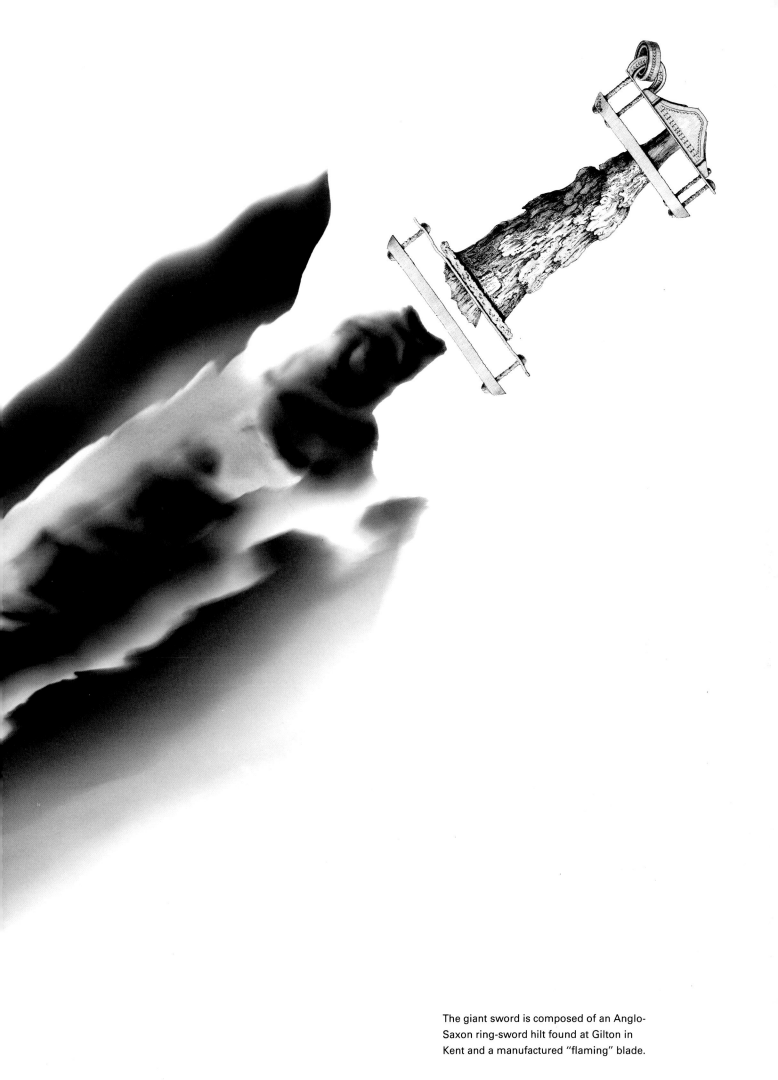

The giant sword is composed of an Anglo-Saxon ring-sword hilt found at Gilton in Kent and a manufactured "flaming" blade.

He swiftly swings about and slashes,
Striking up music on her skull;
But Hrunting's famous edge has failed,
This battleflame won't bite, won't burn.
The Geat is hurt as if a god
Had failed him, but he throws his fear
And Hrunting, glory gone, to the ground,
Trusting the strength he stores in fingers.
But so gigantic is the stench
Of heated, stifling air, so heavy
To breathe, like drinking devil's mead,
That churning nausea almost chokes him.
Fighting the seizure in his stomach,
He grabs her wrist and shoulder, grappling,
Twisting her backward to the floor.
But she all slick with greasy sweat
And strong and quick as seven wildcats
Wrenches free and he starts to fall,
She is upon him, pressing claws
Against his face, knee to his groin,
Him on his back with her astride;
Her heavy, broad-blade knife in hand,
This mother jabs its jagged point
With fury, faster than eye can follow,
Not seeing where she strikes, avenging
Beloved Grendel. The Geat was lost,
But for the tightly ring-locked byrnie
That turns each stroke the troll-wife gives—
That, and the help of holy God.
Beowulf with a madman's will
Whirls his arm like a massive whip,
Smashing her face with knotted fist;
The backswipe knocks her off his body,
Scattering teeth; he jumps up, sees
The blaze of light upon a blade
Nearly hid by a heap of armor,
Leaps for it, fearing for his life,
Seizes it—such a sword no man
But Beowulf could wield, so vast!—
And in a single arc he sweeps it
Up from the ground against her throat
And through, it breaks the bone-rings, passes
Through air, then back to bite the ground.
Her body topples. Beowulf,
Propped on the blood-dark blade, exults,
Thanks God for lighting him to life.

He looked around. The rotting bodies,
At different stages, turned his stomach
Again; he retched, but rage had likewise
Seized him, drove him to search for something.
At last he saw, along the wall,
Apart from all the bodies piled
Like cords of wood, the corpse of Grendel.
He strode across through smoky firelight

Hefting the sword by hilt and blade,
His mind a black blur of revenge.
He paused before he fixed both hands
To hilt and raised it, thinking how
This brute had slaughtered sleeping men,
So many—carried to his cave
These corpses, half decayed, half eaten.
All his hatred went to his hands.
The trunk bounded wide at the blow,
The loose head rolled along the floor.
But then a wonder! Beowulf
Watched the great sword begin to wane:
Its blade was melting, making shapes
Like icicles, as when the cold
Loosens in spring, the Lord undoing
The steely locks on streams and lakes;
The figured blade had burned away—
So hot the blood, so harsh the venom
Brewed in the kin of Cain that died.
He left—who would linger in hell?—
Quickly, taking none of the treasure
Heaped on the floor and hung on walls,
But only Grendel's great grim head,
The hilt without a blade, and Hrunting.
He clove the water cleanly upward,
Having cleansed it with goodly killing.

Long had the pool been closed on him, and still.
It seemed a tomb. The Dane and all the men
Sat gazing at it. One said, "strength and will
Are not enough. We'll not see him again."
And others: "even heroes must have air";
"Madness to hunt that seawolf in her lair."

It was the Danes who talked; the Geats sat dumb.
Hrothgar at last stood up and firmly said,
And sadly, "Beowulf will never come."
The Danes went home. For Geats, all hope was dead;
They merely wished. Perhaps a shaft of air. . . .
Nothing to do but sit and sickly stare

At water.
             All at once the water burst
Into a dome of shining spray and steel
And blood, and something hairy, half immersed—
Coming shoreward! No time to think or feel;
They gaped. Then Beowulf was standing there,
Raising the head of Grendel by its hair.

Stumbling, yelling, laughing, they rushed to him
And quickly loosened helm and byrnie, seeing
How rings of mail had punched into his skin,
How claws had scored his cheeks. Like some strange being
He seemed, with something frightful in his eyes.
The dark pool swirled with blood below dark skies.

Forth they quickly fared on the path—no need
To linger! Four men, sweating, bore the spear
That skewered Grendel's head. They crossed the mead
Where they had raced their horses, now all clear
Of snow, and reached the stone-bright path. The sight
Of Hart was golden in the noonday light.

Beowulf yanked the spear out, grasped the hair,
And followed by his men went through the door
Hefting the head. The Danes were sitting there,
Drinking. Wordless he flung it to the floor,
And as it rolled he greeted Hrothgar, who,
Like Wealhtheow, stared. What could they say or do?

"*Wes hael* my faithful friends, Hrothgar and all!
Much I regret this marring of your pleasure,
This crude disturbance of your clashing cups
By thumping down that thing amidst your drinking—
But such a head is heavy, so I dropped it.
I'm sorry, too, my gift is so unsightly
With clots of blood, and blackening already;
Not the best way to please my lady Wealhtheow!
Well may you stare; you've never seen him close;
But I, I've even met the mother, less
Mild than Grendel in mood, and better armed.
She would have killed me like a little calf,
But for God and my byrnie. Hrunting, though:
Fine sword to handle, but for biting skulls
It might as well be made of wood. But God,
Who helps the needy, showed me near the wall
The glitter of a giant sword. I grabbed it,
Killed her, and hacked off Grendel's head. But so
Strong was the blood, the blade has melted. Here,
Then, is a second gift, the golden hilt.
The head's a better trophy than the hand,
Though it would look less handsome than the hart's
Up on your gable. And another gift:
All of you now can sleep at Hart, and soundly."

Beowulf's smile was hurtful to endure,
A twisting of the lips alone. His eyes
Reflected pale blue light as still and pure
As that of some deep vein of hidden ice
Opened to view. The Dane, uneasy, gazed
Down at the hilt; he wished to be amazed.

And it was splendid: handle serpent-wrought,
Showing the flood that slew the giant-race
Back at the world's beginning, those who fought
The will of God; an ocean took their place.
The cross-piece, cut with narrow runes, displayed
His name who had this wonder-weapon made.

Hrothgar had heard of God, and of the soul—
A kind of deathless bird which no one sees,
Living within your breast, which takes a toll
From all you do and think, which you must please
At risk of endless torture after death,
Which flees your body at your final breath.

You wear a cross, a soul-mark, on your neck
The way you'd wear a noose. No ornament,
No ghostly symbol, this. Against the wreck
Of hopes and hall-joys, life that's merely lent,
Cut by sword-edge, sickness, or foul old age,
This life of wretched wrongs for which the wage

Is death and greasy rotting down in mud—
Against this world you need a greater force,
A God who pours his friendship free as blood,
The warrior-king from Heaven Hall whose source
Of strength and wealth gushes forever, killed
On cross then rising till his power filled

The universe. For Christ was on the rood
And then his rood, bejewelled, rose in the sky
Like northern lights. He gave his flesh as food,
His blood as drink, and then, since still we die,
His gallows-tree as passage from the grave
For all like him—the strong, the good, the brave.

Hrothgar had heard what Edwin later knew,
And Coifi, when out of night and back to night
From end to end of the hall a swallow flew,
Spending a heart-beat in the warmth and light:
"That was our life—one moment out of grim
Darkness. If Christ can help, I'll follow him!"

Thinking these solemn things while gazing spellbound
Down at the hilt by firelight, Hrothgar spoke,
Lifting his eyes at last and talking slowly:
"God's work and yours, dear Beowulf, be praised!
And endless thanks for bringing us this booty,
This head, and with it peace to Hart forever.
Who'd think a man could breathe within that mere?
I've searched but cannot find the words to fit
Your deeds, for there are none and never will be.
Still, I can clearly say that God is with you,
And therefore you are better than us all;
And that your glory-fame will cross the flood-ways,
My dear friend Beowulf, to distant lands,

To every land. Don't threaten it with looseness!
Be steadfast in your strength. I will be helpful,
Showing my friendship for you, as I've pledged.
And long will you be helpful in your land.
Unlike Heremod. Raven-like his soul,
And wolfish grew his thoughts; he gave no rings,
This prince of Danes, as love and duty bid.
No, and he butchered them, his best of friends,
His mead-companions, fellow fighting-men!
At last he went alone, far from the joy
Of mead-halls, gifted though he was by God
With strength and valor much beyond all men.
Now he endures his due in hell forever.
Take warning, Beowulf, from Heremod!
I speak as one who's lived for many winters.

For pride of life can lull the soul to sleep.
You think the world is waiting on your will,
That wealth and strength and youth are yours forever;
Then that your goods from God are all too little.
By steps the devil has you do his will.
Fearless at last, you rob and kill your friends.
Beware of wickedness, dear Beowulf,
That after death will send your soul to torture!
You will be strong and young a little while;
But sooner than you care to reckon, sickness
Or sword will cut you off from youth and strength—
Or arrow, fire, or flood; or loathesome age
Will make your face go slack, your spittle run.
Your eyes and breath will break, and death will have you.

I know of youth and age and death. For years
I wielded power on middle-earth, so widely
Across this world, so well with edge and ash-spear,
I never feared, or thought I'd have, a foe.
All of that quickly changed with Grendel's coming.
Now thank the Lord that I have lived to see
His gory, rotting head roll on my floor!
And now to table—treasure-giving tomorrow."

So Beowulf went quickly to his seat,
His face at ease; they feasted as before,
Till night. Then Hrothgar rose and yawned; the Geat,
Glazed with fatigue, moved likewise toward the door,
But someone showed him up to Hrothgar's loft,
Where, till the dawn-birds called, his bed was soft.

Morning: the acrid scent of dampened ashes,
Shy ghost of light through roof- and window-holes;
Meat, beer, and bread are set with blunted crashes
On boards for breakfast; everyone unrolls.
To pass the night is still to pass a test,
Even with Grendel dead. They sleep all dressed,

Though not like others braced upright in chairs
Asleep in armor, sword or axe on knees,
Ready to rush at trolls got up as bears.
No, if these men are never quite at ease
They're only part-time killers, for at night
Mostly they stop. And now they greet the bright

Beacon of God that through the opened door
Shatters the beer-fume darkness with its beams,
Scouring the puddled, crust- and bone-foul floor,
Sending the mob of phantoms loosed by dreams
Back to their lair. The door's now open wide;
One mumbling at the others walks outside–

Unferth, stepping behind a tree. At leisure
He sees against the sodden, grey-brown hills
How little snow the sun turns up, a measure
Of how far spring has come.... a sword-clank chills
His heart, he wheels; an errand-man, with blade
Reversed, commends him for the loan he'd made

And hands him Hrunting. Beowulf appears
And shakes his hand in thanks. Unferth, relieved,
Remembering how well his Hrunting shears
Not bone but wool, is like a man reprieved.–
Geats are bent on leaving, not lingering.
Their prince re-enters Hart and greets the king:

"The time has come to tell you we must go,
Hrothgar; we wish to seek out Higelac
Across the sea the way we came. At Hart
We have been welcome to your wealth and food
And drink, and you have let me do such deeds
As live forever. Much I've learned from that.
If ever I can gain yet greater love
From you than now, with works of war, I'm ready;
If ever from abroad I hear of foes–
As happened once–attacking you, I'll help,
I'll bring a thousand thanes to fight your war!
I know that Higelac though young will help me,
With men and words and works, to honor you.
And Hrethric Hrothgarsson: if he decides
To visit us, he'll find there many friends.
Travel is good for men whose worth is much."

Then Hrothgar, smiling broadly, answered him:
"Only our God could send such golden language!
I've never heard a man so young whose mind
Could work so fast, so well! You're strong in body,
Wise in thinking, wonderful as word-smith.

I'll say, if sword or sickness takes your leader,
And you're not dead, the Geats could do no better
Than call you to be king, if you are willing.
The longer you've been here, the more I've liked
Your spirit, Beowulf, dear son! Your deeds
Have forged our friendship; there will be no feuding
For Geats and Danes, and while I wield this kingdom
The ring-stem boats will cross the gannet's bath,
Bearing to you their fill of friends and treasure.
We'll take our stand—toward friend, toward foe—together.
Many the times we'll meet again, dear prince."

But you could see in spite of hopeful speech
How Hrothgar felt, and what he truly thought,
As he commanded Danes to take to the beach
The twelve rich gifts for Beowulf, and sought
To cheerily bid him take the dolphin-track
And find his well-loved kin, but soon come back:

He kissed dear Beowulf, embraced his neck,
The tear-flow glistening on his grizzled beard—
He hoped but, wise and old, did not expect
That they would meet again. And as they neared
The beach, this king—peerless till age at length
Stripped him like others of the joys of strength—

Saw that the Geat was happy. He indeed,
Treading the turf now springy with its grass,
Was thinking of the golden cups of mead
Waiting in Geatland, of the golden mass
Of treasure he had gained, of tales to tell.
Yes, he had saved the Danes, had done it well.

They came in jingling chain-mail, many men,
To where the fresh-tarred boat at anchor rode.
The coastguard, high above them, once again
Rode down; but now he paused, watching them load
The boat with horse and treasure—not the same
As when he'd shaken his spear at those who came

Unknown, unasked! He bid the Geat goodbye
And got from him a sword inlaid with gold
That set his worth at mead-bench ever high.
Beowulf, homeward-eager, stooped to hold
Briefly the hands of Hrothgar, Wealhtheow, then
Lightly leaping aboard rejoined his men

Beowulf sails home. The prow is from the
Oseberg ship. In the background is the rocky
archipelago on the west coast of Sweden
which we imagine as Beowulf's destination.

Beside the mast, as good friends pushed them off.
Deep water now. They left the land of Danes. –
Only one bailed, none rowed; the winds aloft
Hollowed the sail as thick ropes coped with strains;
The sea-wood creaked. A cloud will scud on the sky
No swifter than their longboat seemed to fly,

Their foamy-throated beauty, on the blue.
Beowulf stayed amidships by the mast –
And treasure – till the seacliffs came in view,
Familiar Geatish headlands: home at last.
The bow-taut stem, urged by the wind, struck sand
Suddenly. Beowulf, the first on land,

Saw someone running shouting down to meet them.
The watch, who'd stared at sea so long, embraced
The prince, then others, taking care to greet them
For Higelac. And with some help he placed
Two anchors deep in sand to moor the boat,
Tying the dragon-vessel by its throat,

Making it safe from surf, and had some men
Unload the cargo, take it to the hall.
Then briskly, glad to be on land again,
They walked to where it lay, behind a wall
Of sharpened stakes five minutes from the shore.
Beowulf sadly felt that nevermore

Could Higelac's seem the finest hall on earth,
As he approached it on a path of planks:
But all the greater seemed to him its worth,
For he was guardian here. He breathed out thanks
To God for fragrant woodsmoke curling, proof
Of hall-joy, from the center of the roof.

For all this fairest folk, the king and queen
And thanes, were happy; Higelac was young
And Hygd a girl of only seventeen
(She was no Thryth, whose lovers' necks were wrung
Till Offa tamed her; they should weave the peace,
Lovely ladies, not slaughter men like geese!).

From the interior of the Ror Ege, looking
toward islands of the Weder Island Fjord.

Beowulf pushed the door aside and sniffed
With joy the firelit dark: yes, he was back.
With crashing benches, all stood up to lift
Their cups and shout; and up sprang Higelac,
Who little loved to lie or sit too long,
Shoved his way to his nephew through the throng—

He had been told that Beowulf was back—
And brought him arm in arm to where he'd made,
Beside his own, a place where he would lack
Nothing. Beowulf bowed to Hygd, arrayed
In garnet-studded silk, who gave him mead
In gold and kissed him; then he took the lead,

Giving Hrothgar's greeting to Higelac
And adding, "here's my place, dear Higelac;
God in his love has brought me back to you."
The Geat-king nearly broke to know what happened:
"Now tell us what you did among the Danes!
What came of your so sudden need to seek,
Across the sea, to kill that foreign monster?
Did you relieve poor Hrothgar's lot at all?
I've been washed in a sea of fears and worries.
I tried for long to tell you, let the Danes
Themselves deal with their Danish Grendel-fiend,
Not you! God knows, we've pain enough unasked.
But now at last, thank God! you're home alive."

Beowulf settled, mead in hand, and spoke:
"After we landed, stiff with frozen sea-salt,
They took us right to Hrothgar and the Hall,
To Hart, a big place bright with gold and color
But not well kept inside, too dank, too cold.
Still, they were glad to see me—gave us drink,
The best, for much had Hrothgar heard of me,
He knew my father, not the least of men,
Had heard of what my hands could do. He hoped;
And told me I could meet the troll that night.
He gave me by his son the seat of honor,
But still I had to hear the lies of Unferth,
That brother-killer—calling me a liar,
Almost! I would have hurt him, but for Hrothgar.
Instead, I silenced him by silencing
The monster. Through the dark he came. The Danes
Had left. We guarded Hart alone, and waited.—
The door snapped open. But he blocked the moonlight,
I couldn't see him. Suddenly he stooped,
Butchered Hondscio, and gorged—I had to listen!
And wait till he was deep within the hall.
Next, with a giant body-bag in hand,
He bent toward me; but I had better plans
Than being hauled, fresh meat, to Grendel's hole.
I took his arm in both my hands and twisted.
What an uproar! I felt my fingers press
Through parting, slipping sinews to the bone,

Entering Higelac's hall:
door of the Tuft stave church, Sandver.

As hands and will both tightened on the task.
He got away, went wailing through the night,
A squealing wail, like giant hogs when slaughtered.
I'd ripped his arm off—hung it up on Hart.
I'd failed, had meant to kill him on the floor,
Where he killed Danes. He got to die at home."

The hall was silent, Higelac not drinking,
Hygd's eyes fixed on the face of Beowulf.

"In the morning they cleaned and mended Hart.
The livelong day we had a Danish feast—
I've never seen such hall-joy under heaven!
Barrels of wine and mead to wet the food down,
Meats and cakes to cram the bellies of hundreds!
Queen Wealhtheow, handsome lady, went around
With cup in hand, encouraged us to eat,
To drink, as if the Danes and Geats were timid!
And Freawaru, flax-haired, lovely daughter,
Gracefully passed the beer to men on benches.
And Aescher told the tale of Finn and Hnaef,
The thane that Hrothgar loved unlocked his word-hoard
Soon to be shut forever, told of slaughter,
Of Finn who came to kill his guests by night,
Of Hnaef who died, and Hengest his avenger
Brooding all winter, marking Finn for murder—
Little good had it done the Danes and Frisians
For Hildeburh, the sister of Hnaef the Dane,
To marry Finn to stop their ancient feud.
And so—you mark my words!—the marriage-plans
Of Hrothgar will be vain, be wrecked by vengeance.
For Freawaru is to wed young Ingeld,
Prince of the Heathobards that Danes all hate.
One day at beer, while Danes are visiting,
A grim old spearsman who's forgotten nothing
Will tap the prince's shoulder, talking softly:
'You see that Dane? The sword he's wearing—know it?
You should. He got it from your father—not,
I think, a gift. It's sad, how blood runs thin
In families. Here's the man who slaughtered Froda,
Strutting around your palace with the sword
That you should have by rights. How really sad.'
And then the oaths on both sides will be broken!
When princes fall, it's seldom steel lies still
For long, however beautiful the bride."

Beowulf tipped his mead-cup bottom up,
Paused to let out his breath and wipe his lips,
Then staring at the fire continued speaking:
"That night, with drunken Danes all sleeping, Aescher
Was killed. The mother had come, and I was elsewhere.
We couldn't even burn the body—gone,
Dragged under water by the devil-woman
Getting even for Grendel. So the king
Asked me to pay that demon back for Aescher.

Recalling the fight with Grendel's mother.

82

All went together to the Grendel-pool.
Going down in the water wasn't hard—
I'd done that—but I had to wait for her;
So, drifting in the dark and silent water,
I couldn't even fix my will on catching,
Then killing! Nothing in that numbing water
For eye or hand or will to hold to! When,
At last, she pulled me through the hole—such light
Of fire on gold and steel and brilliant stones,
Her body like a wildcat's, horrid beauty—
I knew that I was not my own but hers,
Unless God helped. The horror! and the stench:
Friends, I have seen myself as dead and rotting.
Many have died; but if one moment, truly
You look on death, on what it is to die—"
Wordless he sat there, man of swords and words.

Not even candle-flames were flickering.

"And then I saw the massive Weland-sword
And sliced the creature's head off. Now I'm here."

Then he stood up, and pointing out to them
The treasures by the door, addressed them all
But mostly Higelac: "you see what Hrothgar,
Grateful for what I did, has given me:
A helmet, boar's head banner, heirloom sword,
Byrnie he got from Heorogar the king
But didn't wish to pass to Heoroward,
His heir, although he loved the lad; and rings
And vessels fat with gold; and finest horses,
Four of them, fallow-colored, in the courtyard.
As Hrothgar gave me this, so, Higelac,
I give it all to you, and gratefully.
For who's my kin, dear Higelac, apart
From you? Enjoy these gifts, and use them well."

Though all the gifts were Higelac's, I heard
The hero went to Hygd, and on her breast,
Around her neck, he placed without a word
The necklace Wealhtheow gave to him, the best,
The richest, since the Brosings'. From that day
She wore it always, till it went away

With Higelac to Frisia where he died,
Years later. Now, he brought a gold-hilt sword
For Beowulf, and bound it to his side;
And as he did so, loudly made him lord
Of vast domaines. Facing the yelling crowd,
Unchanged by what he heard, the young prince bowed.

II. The Years Between

Iron is grey like ice but grimmer;
We give as well as get its hurts.
The sword of a wonder-smith is old.
He had forged it with fire and hammer,
Braided iron rods and beat them,
Making a swirling serpent-blade;
Welded strips of steel for edges,
So fine they'd slice a falling leaf.
Polished, it makes a marbled mirror
Glinting dully as a gravestone.
When slowly taken from a scabbard
Only your spine and stomach hear it.
The blade grows hard with battle-blood.

———————————————

Slowly at first the seasons turned.
After yuletide the year was new
But still the weather of the world
Warred with the iron strength of winter,
Thrusting the frost aside with thaws,
Then silenced by the snow again.
But coldness melted, clouds dispersed,
And spring set in with sweetest airs
From all the flowers dense with fragrance
And birds that sang as they built and mated.
The season would have seemed too brief,
But that it merged with massive summer
Whose slow days last till time for sleep,
Each day afloat on drifts of warmth.
Time was lost in the loosened air,
Dissolved in languid heat and light,
So that the summer seemed forever,
Swelling to autumn, gold and scarlet,
Turning the trees and fields to treasure. . . .
But then the winter-warnings came –
The clench of cold, the cautious light –
Telling autumn to be done,
To ripen fast before the winter.
Then raging sky-winds fought the sun
And leaves were flung from limbs to the ground
Till all was grey that once was green,
And frost at last had locked the earth.
Thus turns the year to yesterdays,
And winter's back, as the world requires.

That was the hero's first year home.

And so it was with Beowulf in youth
Then age. His spring and summer stretched forever,
And yet he knew that Hrothgar spoke the truth
That day—that age if nothing else would sever
His soul from body—for he'd seen the black
Visage of death, and knew it must come back.

Waiting, he felt afloat on youth, which passed
Unmarked. Yet though the old seemed set apart,
Unlike, he knew the truth and held it fast,
And year by year it cooled the young man's heart.—
But in the early years, one dawn in spring,
Higelac felt a surge on wakening:

The streams were gushing, fish were leaping high,
And Higelac must be about his play!
Banging the hall-door open with a cry,
Poised there beaming, "we must be underway!",
He shouted to the men at bread and beer,
"It's Frisia this time!" With a single cheer,

Beating their knife-butts on the boards, they rose
With joy but not surprise—they knew their lord.
Beowulf, with the look of one who knows
Too much, a look at once detached and bored,
Rose too, but slowly. Frisia, fat with trade,
A table ponderous with feast-things, laid

For Higelac, lay open to the sea,
To Higelac. He came within six days.
From hall to hut they took what they could see,
Burning the remnant, stalking through the haze
And screams: from jewels, platters, slaves and swords
And cattle, to the very nails and boards.

As they were loading up, the Franks arrived—
Unheard, with horses and a thousand men.
Higelac, pillaging a hut, survived
Only a minute: out like bull from pen
He rushed at forty Franks, hit one, and reeled
As spears and throwing-axes pierced his shield,

His byrnie, and his tender body.
When swords had drunk of him he died;
They got him on the ground, and hacked.
To fate and to the Franks went all:
His life, his armor, and not least
The necklace Beowulf had brought him
And hung that night on the neck of Hygd.
The prince, in youthful pride, had asked
For trouble; when it came, it took him.

Beowulf, first in fighting always,
Alone before the lance- and spearsmen,
Was not at home in raiding huts;
His place was by his prince's side
When axes shattered shields and bones.
So after taking token plunder,
Some rings, he'd left the peaceful raiding–
No danger–, stood aside, and gazed
Out to the sea.... The tone of screaming
Changing, he saw the sudden Franks;
Dashed in a panic for his prince;
And when he found him fallen, saw
One swordsman, cheered by others, chopping
His neck asunder. Scattering Franks
Like broken teeth, he took the man–
Dayraven, famous for his killing–
In both his hands, then hugged him close,
So close they heard him crack and snap
Like bonfire-twigs, as Beowulf
Instantly broke his bone-house, crushing
To little squeaks his struggling breath.
He dropped the carcass limp as a cloak,
Seized his victim's sword, called Naegling,
And paid attention to the others.
Whirling the brilliant blade so fast
It seemed a blaze of solid light,
He littered the ground with limbs and splinters;
And yet more fearful was his face,
Exalted, hardly human now.
Well he'd repaid his prince in war:
Franks on the ground for treasure given.

But other Franks were fighting well;
So when the cutting-war had stopped,
The field of death was filled with Geats
Plundered of gear by grasping Franks.
Beowulf, last to leave, was backed
Against the sea; he swam in armor,
With loot, to where the longboat waited.
Hangdog the wretched Geats came home
To mourn their king's unburied corpse.

————————————————

When Hygd had tried to give him treasure-rings
And kingship, Heardred being still a child,
Beowulf–knowing well how makeshift-kings
Were tempted to destroy the heirs, beguiled
By power–refused; said he would take no wage
For guarding Heardred till he came of age.

————————————————

Beowulf, settling like a log-built hall
Into himself, had reached his middle years
When Heardred came of age one blazing fall,
A treasure-season, paying the arrears
For several pallid harvests with a wealth
That seemed a pledge to Heardred's future health

And Geatland's too. But Beowulf that day,
Brooding on two successions to the throne
From many years before, was far away
Among the honored dead that he had known.
For he remembered all; and what is past,
He knew, is all of living that will last.

When he was barely seven winters old
His mother's father Hrethel, king of Geats,
Took him from Ecgtheow, gave him clothes and gold
And little weapons, richest wines and meats—
Same as he gave to Haethcyn, Higelac,
And Herebald; and Beowulf gave back

That love that Hrethel shared among the four,
His sons and grandson. Loving one another,
They felt no envy. Therefore all the more
The child had suffered when the middle brother,
Haethcyn, came screaming home one day that year
Babbling of Herebald and blood; in fear

And ticklish grief they rushed to where the boys
Had set up targets for their horn-curved bows
And found the eldest breathing with a noise
Like raven-croaking, in his final throes,
An arrow through the throat; the ground was dark
With spreading blood. Haethcyn had missed his mark.

How could the wailing king of Geatland settle
This death by slaughtering the killer, his son?
Or even hate him, though he liked him little.
And Herebald the bright had been the one
With promise as a king, among the three!
Soon Hrethel died of helpless misery.

It wounded Beowulf, a brooding child,
And made him now, this man of middle years,
This hero of demeanor strangely mild,
Think of a tale he'd heard of hopeless tears
And grief—it often came to him unwilled—
About a man whose only son was killed,

Old man whose son, a youth, was made to ride
The gallows and rot, a joy to jabbing birds.
And he, though strong, was forced to stand aside
And weep the mourning-song, with neither words
To help himself nor deeds to help his son
Whose death was just. The old man's life was done:

Daily he viewed his dead son's dwelling-place,
Its wind-blown roof, its frost-encrusted walls,
No fire with laughter harp and drink, just space
Where snow was sifting. Deaths of men, of halls,
Are much alike. And then he took to bed,
Like Hrethel, wanting only to be dead.

As killing leads to killing, so a thought
Of one death leads to others. Gazing out
At autumn richness, Beowulf, distraught,
Shades of the past and future all about,
Saw death, not wealth—the fate of men. He felt
Its chill; and mostly on the Swedes he dwelt.

Over wide water strife of Swede and Geat,
Surging, recurrent, like the North Sea swell,
Had injured both; but "in the end defeat
Will be for us", he'd felt since Haethcyn fell,
The arrow-heir, himself pierced through and through,
One of many the Swedish raiders slew.

Beowulf heard of that when he was still,
Though strong, not quite a fighting-man: how Swedes—
Onela, Othere—raped and robbed their fill
Near Hresnaberg, sowing the vengeance-seeds.
But it was Ongentheow their father, old
And fierce, who cut down Haethcyn, stretched him cold,

And snatched his queen, stripped of her gold and goods,
Back from the Geats that they had not yet felled,
Then chased this remnant into Ravenswood
And camped outside it. All night long he yelled
Into the hollow woods how he at dawn
Would hang and hack them, for birds to fatten on.

Like Hengest's men at Finnsburg, Geats were ready
To take position at the forest gate
And fight with will and steel both hard and steady.
But just as dawn was darkening their fate
They heard the clang of trumpets—Higelac!
Brief fight, and then the Geats were on the track—

Bloody and wide through field and wood—of Swedes.
Beowulf nearly word-for-word recalled
The tale of Wulf Wanreding, Geatish hero:
"Ongentheow went behind an earthen wall,
A mound, and like a boar he stood at bay,
Fighting for wife and sons and treasure, fiercer
Than ever, white-haired though he was; so when
We swarmed the wall, I marked him out as mine,
Hit him, and saw the spring of blood from veins
Under his hair, but with a howl he sprang,
Chopped through my helmet, ear, and cheek-bone, laughing,
Then turned to face my brother but too late:
From where I lay in pain I watched him shudder

As Eofor's sword went smashing through his shield
And skull, much widening the wound I'd made,
Reaching his life. The old man loosely fell.
When we had beat them, good friends bound my wounds
And got me up, as Eofor grabbed for loot,
Plundered the fierce old Swede of helmet, sword,
And byrnie, but did not expose his body
High on the nearby hill to wolf and raven
Because he'd fought so well. Enough to kill him.
Eofor took the loot to Higelac,
Who took it. In return, when we were home
He gave in thanks a thousand hides of land
To each of us, but something even sweeter
To him: 'my only daughter—take her home'."

Beowulf at the time had loved this tale,
Much told, and other war-tales; on the verge
Of manhood, tougher than his peers like mail
To shirts of wool, he'd felt his muscles surge
When someone spoke of fighting. That was youth.
Now, by himself, he grappled with the truth.

And what was that? He thought of Higelac,
Young uncle, more like brother, made a king
The day that Haethcyn died: he'd not come back
From Frisia twelve years later, in the spring,
The year's and his. Now Heardred takes his place,
As he had taken Haethcyn's, whose disgrace

For killing Herebald the better heir
Was doubled when their father died of grief.
"The truth is endless killing, and despair
From which my death will be the sole relief.
For Heardred will be killed, and then—." They call.
He slowly stood, and made his way to the hall.

————————————————

Heardred was killed the autumn following
By Swedes. (When Othere died of stroke, his heirs
Had been attacked by the usurping king,
Onela, who had trapped them unawares
At home—they hadn't heard their father was dead.
He fired their hall and waited; but they fled

South in the night to Geatland seeking haven.
They got it, and the Geats that very day
Were host to Onela, and every raven
In Geatland made the feast. That was no way
For neighbors to behave!) One Swedish heir,
Eanmund, had long been lying plundered bare,

With Heardred, and the beasts had long begun
Picking and choosing, when with many men
Beowulf came from hunting. What they've done,
He thought, we'll do to them, and they again
To us. —And then a burst of self-disgust!
"The Geats my people, given me in trust,

And while they die, I hunt! Nor was I there
When Higelac was killed. I served the Danes
Far better." And he washed his raw despair
With tears. Those hearing, buffeted their brains
To understand such words and sobs. They failed,
These men who guiltless laughed, and guiltless wailed.

———————————————

Next day they built for Geats and Swede a pyre
That sent the bodies high to heaven—smoke
That fed the clouds. Then moved by old desire,
And duty, Beowulf sought Hygd. They spoke,
Closely. When he was chosen king, his queen
Was Hygd, whose touch was calming and serene.

So Beowulf protected Eadgils,
The heir, to put him on the Swedish throne;
For he had had enough of clashing wills
And swords with Swedes. Since Beowulf alone
Commanded—long the greatest, finally king—
He gave himself entire to everything

That should be tended, nothing that should not,
So proving that his strength and will were led
By wisdom, now. And when at last he fought
Onela, he'd prepared the way (instead,
Like other kings, of lunging like a bear):
He'd found some Swedish friends—tested the air.

Two years to find his Swedish friends
And let them ripen. Then he lunged,
A bear and wolf at once—one bound,
It seemed, from Geatland to the Swedes
By night—and caught them at their cups;
Not bothering to burn the hall,
He thundered toward them through the door
Killing with benches swung like clubs
Or flung like tree-limbs torn in a gale.
The Swedes in horror fled the hall,
Making for Vaener's moonlit ice,
Its fortress on the facing shore,
Followed by Geats like nightmare-figures
Hurling their spears and fearful screams.
Beowulf leaped for Onela;
Sliding the ice propelled by spears,

One in each hand, he gave a heave
And as he coasted cast them both—
They crossed inside the Swedish king.

So Beowulf had had his will:
The son of Othere sat enthroned.
But Eadgils seemed among these Swedes,
His people, strangely sullen, thankless.
Beowulf noticed this and never,
In all his life, forgot that look.

———————————————

Some twenty years of ordered calm had passed
Since Beowulf and Hygd began to reign,
Each year a little shorter than the last.
He now had aged in years—not brawn or brain—
Like Hrothgar when he'd saved him. Slightly blurred
In outline, no less firm of hand and word,

He was an oak that grew more hard with time;
She was a harvest rose whose sweetness grew
More concentrated. Like two words that rhyme
They worked together. Geats no longer slew
Their neighbors, or were slain, yet got their fill
Of drink and meat. So all was well, until

That night of winter when the end began.
King and queen, in their bower, heard a roar
Like giant breath and grinding files; a man
Screamed and his scream kept rising. From the door
They saw what no one could have guessed, a wonder
Like lightning in the snow, and flying thunder:

A fire is moving just above the rows
Of huts, flicking, dipping—and something black
Even against the darkness; from it flows
The fire, with all the while that throbbing clack,
Metallic, screeching! Snow is steamed from roofs,
Thatch is ablaze, the fire tongue-like moves

To lick at people running like maddened ants,
Fleeing their huts, but nowhere can they flee—
People and horses shriek as flames advance
Through all the village. By its light they see,
At last, a monstrous batlike shape in flight
Veering beyond the glow, received by night.

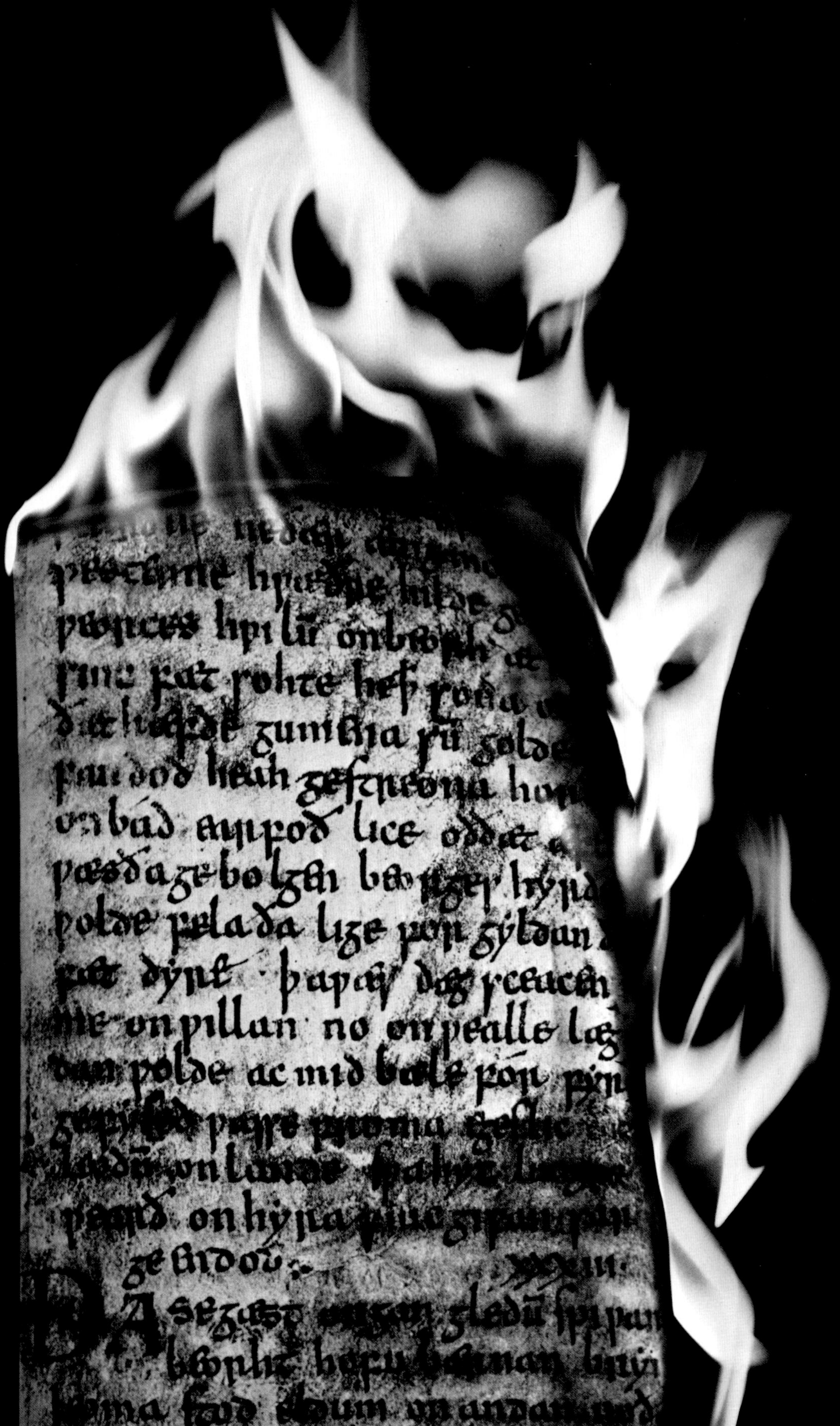

It was all over. Beowulf and Hygd
Herded the Geats, making them save the hall—
Thick logs are slow to burn. Rushing to feed
That fire with snow they gained a home, for all,
Or nearly, now were roofless. Daylight came
Darker than night to show them what the flame,

Thrown from the bat-thing in a gush, had done:
Black holes where huts had been, and on the ground
Hairless greasy bodies, their faces gone,
Their hands and feet burned off, all blackened-browned,
Elbows and knees drawn up—like roasted birds,
All sizes. – Men approached, to have some words

With Beowulf, whose breast within him welled
With darkest thoughts, the sort he'd never known.
(Why this? Had he unwittingly rebelled
Against the Lord? His guilty mood had grown
Till like the smoke it seemed to fill the sky.)
His thane hauled forth a slave who started to cry.

Wiglaf began: "I've got the cause right here.
I'd whipped this boy; he ran away to hide
And came upon a cave inside the mound
Up on the Hron-ness heath where no one goes.
Inside, his fingers touched on things like treasures,
But then he heard a heavy breathing-sound
From deeper in; he grabbed this golden cup
And fled in terror. Seeing how fine it is,
He thought to appease my anger with a present.
His present is the burning of our people!
For what the thief heard breathing in the barrow
Is what has breathed out fire to overwhelm us—
The treasure-guardian, jealous of its gold."

Beowulf: "Tell the weapon-smith
To make me for my fight today
A full-length shield with iron face
And wood and leather backing, laced
With thongs so thick they'll stand the strain
As I move the shield to meet those flames.
Also a spear some twelve feet long.
And instantly. Revenge for wrongs,
These wrongs, is not to be delayed.
This wretched slave will lead the way."

And so he did. The weapon-smith was fast;
Three swordsmen bore the shield and two the spear,
A sixth took Naegling. Twelve in all, they passed
Through heath behind the slave, who wept for fear,
Beowulf thinking of another time
He'd walked through moorland to avenge a crime.

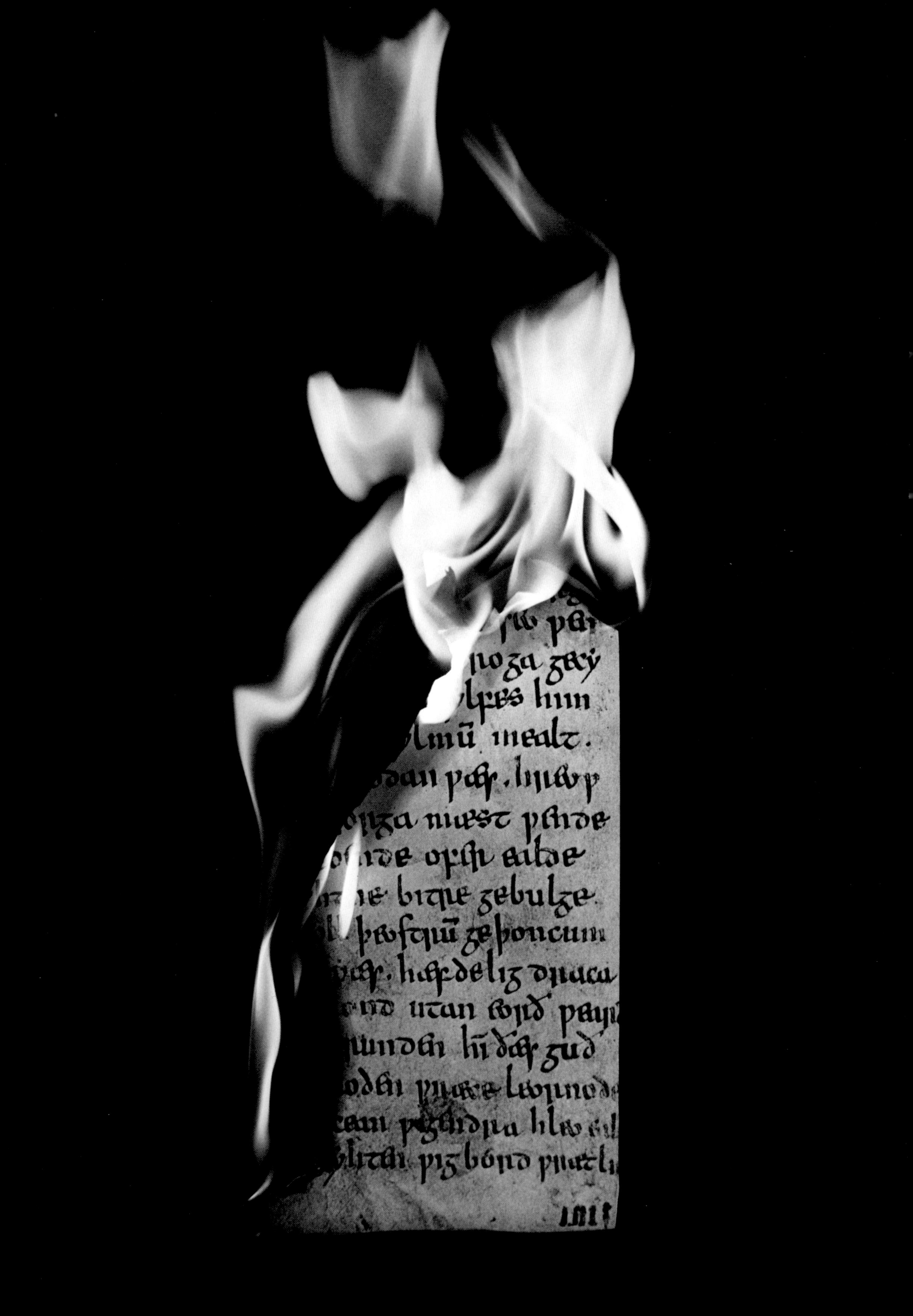

Near where the earth-rim stopped, they saw the barrow,
A mound of furze. Beyond it far below
Was rocky surf, wrinkles of grey and white.
Beowulf watched the hillock, humped and swollen
As if the earth were sick, for signs of movement
There where the slave had pointed to the path
That led down in. Then sitting on a stone
He wrapped a thick dark cloak of thought about him.
Killing the Grendel-race and cleansing Hart,
War against men—he'd never failed. But might have.
The fight in the Grendel-cave had made that clear.
His forehead in his hands, he felt the nearness
Of fate, which moves the stars about the sky.
If God but stood aside, his fate was death.
What he could do, he would: put forth his will,
His strength, like fully tightening his fingers;
And God would act, or not. He got to his feet:

"I've lived through many wars in youth, did marvels
 Of fighting; yet I mean to do one more
 Before the end, if I can force that thing,
 That creature in the treasure-cave, to meet me.
 I take against it sword and spear and byrnie,
 And shield; I cannot face its jets of fire
 Unarmed, with naked hand. But I will not
 Flee it a single foot! Now you move off,
 Wait on that hill till one of us is dead;
 For this is not your fate, this fight is mine
 Alone. I'll win the gold, or die in war."

He said farewell to each man singly, walked
Close to the hole, and called "come out!" in a voice
To grip the dead. He went to greet his fate.

sprece purroe pæl bla

þ hedæᵹ hpila ჳ dnozeli hie

da pæs aull scacen dozol

mete neah nuic suna m

ჳud ჳepædu þahime

III. Last Things

Under a rock-ledge Beowulf was lying
Where Wiglaf in the end had carried him.
He'd walked nine steps and fallen; he was dying.
Venom was in his veins, and every limb
Was burned. But Wiglaf, watering his face
And wounds, had found this sheltered snow-free place

And given him the herbal drink he'd brought
For dulling pain; so Beowulf, at ease
Almost, not talking, moved from thought to thought
Like watching pictures pass. Such dying frees
The mind. The dragon lay not far below,
A twisted smudge upon a sheet of snow.

That stream of fire from the cavern-hole,
Then from the creature's mouth; then scaly coils
Unwinding from the bowels of the barrow.
The soot-black wings outstretched on pointed bones.
Slow on the ground, more bat than snake, but coiling
Quickly together, springing suddenly up.
Fire. A blast that with the force of water
Falls on my shield, I feel my forearm sizzle.

Bright on the bone his sword had bit more weakly
Than he could wish. His wounds began to swell.
Venom was at his heart, his boiling veins
Cracked with his soul-gore.
                      Sometime early on,
Nine thanes, his favorites, following the slave,
Found they could watch things better from the forest
And fled. But Wiglaf ran the other way.
Sheltered behind the shield of Beowulf,
Mindful of what he'd boasted in the mead-hall—
How he would never leave his lord at need—
He paid the Geat-king for his many gifts,
Returning blood for wine, and well-aimed steel
For gold, his battle-mood too hard to melt.
Wiglaf and Beowulf were battle-brothers
Like Wulf and Eofor, but what they fought
Was no mere man or beast, was nothing else
Than that which comes for each of us, the killer,
The final mindless foe. For in the end
The serpent does encircle middle-earth
And wraps us all in darkness, where we die.
This lesser worm is one with that which stills
Our world, and Beowulf is one with us—
Like Wiglaf, and the thanes and slave who thought
They could escape. Their time had not yet come.

The heat. Ordeal by fire. I did no crime,
Why the ordeal? My duty. Killing Grendel.
But now no joy. A shield that burns my knuckles,
No shield. The stroke that shatters Naegling, skull-stroke.
Shivers along my forearm, let it go,
Let go of Naegling and the Geats my people.
Never when young that sword-shock, I was strong.

Thus like a water-coolness came the soothing:
He knew at last that it was not his duty
To save the Geats, but to have strained his will
With all its strength to save them. That he'd done.

Life is on loan, and with the light all life
Will go at last. Ah Wiglaf hit him low! –
That belly-gash will spill his guts – and now
Straight to the mouth my giant spear, I cross
My spear with a flame that lunges forth like swords –
It lessens. Twitching snake-shape loosens. Heat.
Drawing my sax to slice the thing in two.
Like slicing swampwood. Heat. My blood is seething.
But I have done what I could do. No more.

He woke. His swollen limbs were burned to bark
And yet he propped his back against the rock,
Gazing where doorway-lintels framed the dark
Of the cave that held the hoard. He wished to talk.
Wiglaf in joy undid his helm, to lave him
Afresh, both face and limbs, perhaps to save him –

But Beowulf knew better. Braced
Against the cliff, he turned his face
Toward truth as he had turned toward treasure:
His days had stopped, and all his pleasures
Were past, for death was now so close,
Immeasurably close. He spoke:
"Now I would give my son my weapons
And war-dress, but the will of heaven
Gave me no heirloom-guard – no heir
After the flesh.
                    Not once they dared
Attack me, kings that ring us round,
Or try with threats to put us down,
All the winters I held my people
In hand. I did not hold them weakly.
And now I see I used my force
First for sheer joy but then for us,
The Geats. For Hrothgar too, my friend.
I lost that joy in Grendel's den;
Afterwards did my duty, shaped
My will to fit the will of fate.
I never looked for fighting, never
Betrayed my word. And now my pleasure,
Here in my agony, is this:

That at the moment when I slip
Into the void, the Lord of men
Can't blame me for the killing of kin.

Wiglaf my help, my friend, now go,
Quickly. The serpent's dead. Get gold!
And gems! Ransack the treasure-hoard,
So I can look at some and hold
Some in my hands to feel how bright,
How weighty it is, then leave this life
And people I have kept so long
All the more softly. Quick—be gone!"

Wiglaf found some deadwood, ran down the hill,
Pausing to dip it in a pool of fire
Dribbled from monstrous jaws. Poised on the sill
Before the blackness, as he lifted higher
His torch inside the stone-cut vault, he saw
Such sights as stopped, briefly, his heart with awe:

Up on the wall was fixed a gilded standard,
So bright it flashed the torch across the floor
And Wiglaf shut his eyes forever branded
By blue-red-amber brilliance from the store
Of jewels strewn like pebbles on a beach.
He looked again: all was within his reach!

Gold on the ground and wonders on the wall!
And placed by walls were flagons, beakers, plate
(Many a man however wise will fall
Snared by the spell of gold like this, like fate).
But hung and propped were byrnies stiff with rust
And rust-dulled swords, and helmets in the dust.

Grief thrilled him like a spear. He spoke aloud:
"So long ago they lived! Their time is gone,
The helm of night has hidden them, their lives
Are now as if they never had been born.
They died in war, at sea, from age or sickness,
A meal at last for wolves or worms or fish.
And no one's left to tend their byrnies now,
And swords, to polish them and all this silver
Duller than stone. The polishers are dead,
The spearsmen too; these tarnished drinking-cups
Will not offend, no more than crumbling mail
That iron bit yet never broke, or helmets
Hard but adorned with dainty shapes of gold,
All rusted now, just as the men have rotted.
No wine-joy now, or harp, or favorite hawk
Swooping from hall-beams, or the racing-stallion
Stamping in the courtyard. Will nothing stay?
No, for this life is lent: our friends, our kin,
Our goods, our selves, and all this solid earth—
All but eternal treasure, gems and gold—
Are lent for a little time, then turn to nothing."

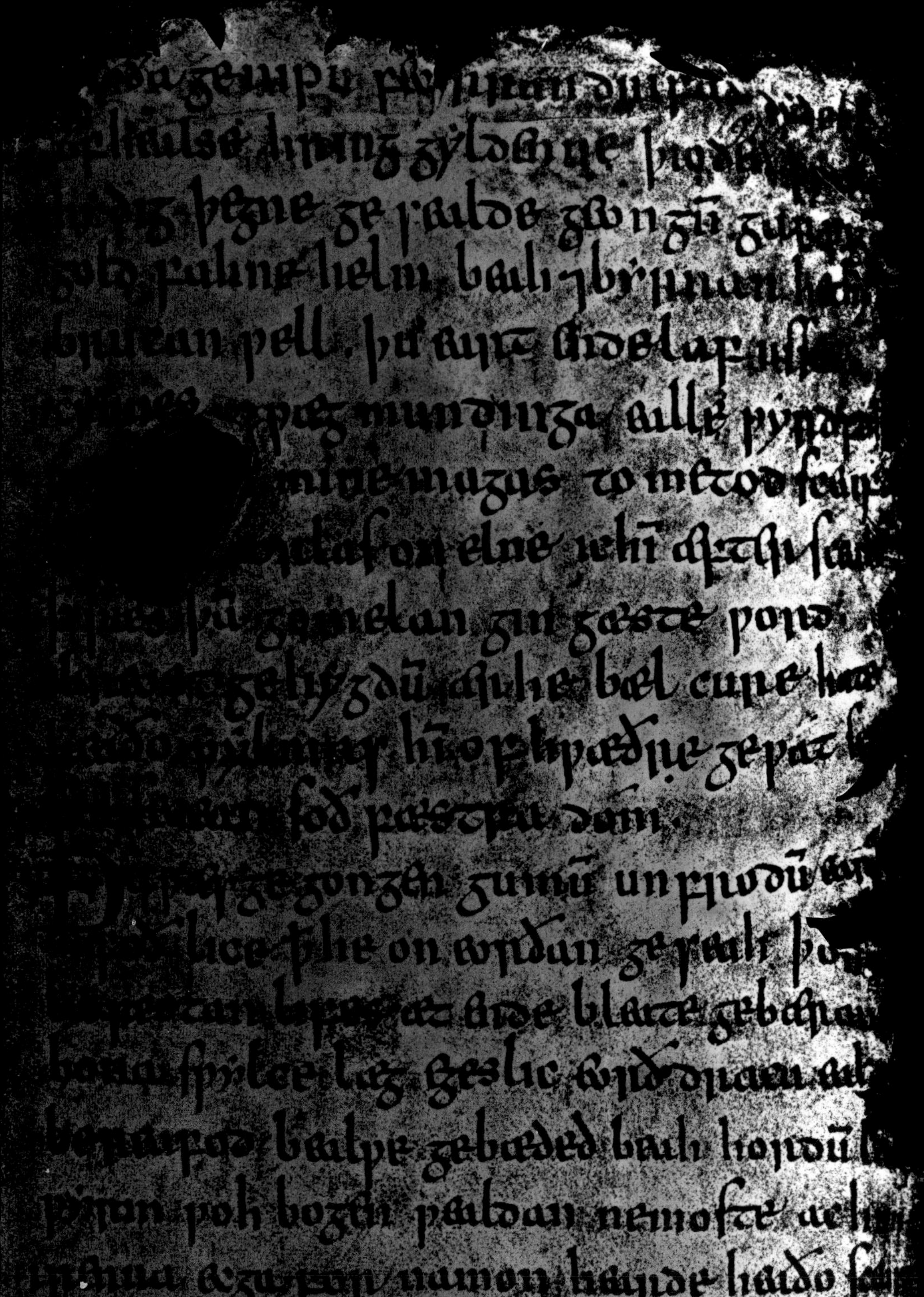

So too the dragon that had found this hoard
Hid by the vanished men—it too had passed,
Killed by heroes with heart and spear and sword.
But what it'd guarded ages long would last—
The glinting treasure, which had lain in wait
For beast and man, strong and deadly as fate.

Now Wiglaf gathered all that he could hold:
The standard; dishes, jewels, cups, a sword;
Then strung his arms with rings of twisted gold
And hurried, wondering if he'd find his lord
Alive. He found him slumped, his eyes half glazed,
His breathing hoarse. He splashed his burns then raised,

Gently, his head. The dying hero spoke,
Looking on the treasures: "I thank the Lord
That I could get these goods and look at them
Before I died, can give them to my folk.
They're bought with life; I cannot be here long.
The venom bites my blood, my limbs are crisp.
But even if my brain had burned, at last
I would have thrust my longspear through those teeth!

Tell them to make a mound atop the headland,
After my body-burning, overlooking
The sea. And let it for my people lift
High and bright above Hron-ness in remembrance,
So that forever after, sailing-men
Will call it Beowulf's Barrow, when the longships
Come from afar across the mist-hung seas."

He took the golden ring from round his neck,
Slowly, and gave it to the strong young spearsman,
His thane; and gave as well his gold-set helmet,
Byrnie, and sword, and said to use them well—:

"Wiglaf, you are the last of the Waegmundings,
My family. All the others fate swept off,
Felled in their strength. And I must follow them."

He spoke no more; his soul was like a place
Entirely filled with light, nothing but light—
Wholly empty and wholly full, bright space—
Or like the same place filled with perfect night.
He entered now the greater emptiness
Of death—and greater fullness of God no less.

Before too long the ten who broke their word,
The battle-weaklings, left their safer ground,
Wearing the shields and weapons they'd preferred
To keep unscathed. They came like beaten hounds
And looked at Wiglaf as, again and again,
He tried with water to wake his lord—in vain.

And then he saw them. Lifting eyes
Reddened with grief and hate, he tried
To steady his voice as he got up
And spoke: "you've come, suddenly struck
By the suspicion that your lord
Might need you. And as if for war—
With helms and byrnies, swords and spears.
Well, he who gave you all that gear
You're standing in—if you will pardon
The truth—, who thought he'd found the hardest,
Bravest fighters around, and gave
At mead-bench weapons in exchange
For pledges of your help in battle,
Your faith to him: well he has sadly,
Entirely thrown away good things,
Like serving roasted boar with cream
To dogs! For trouble came. You showed
Your faith. It's little cause to boast
Of you that Beowulf would have.
But God saw fit to let him stab
The monster through the mouth; alone
He venged himself. And I too showed
My faith; I shielded him too little,
But saw the dragon's fire dwindle
After my gut-thrust.
                              You like peace;
You don't like fighting. Is *defeat*
A better word for what you like?
For when they hear about your flight,
Your visit to the peaceful woods
While Beowulf was killed, our good
And eager neighbors—Frisians, Franks,
Especially the Swedes—will thank
Not gods but you, who've shown how much
They truly have to fear from us.
I will be king; my father killed
The well-loved brother of Eadgils,
The king of Swedes. You understand?
You know by how much, man for man,
The Swedes outnumber us? If not,
You will find out. This peace will stop
Faster than truce at Finnsburh, faster
Than woven peace that little lasted
Between the Heathobards and Danes.
Then spears will fly! and no more strain
Of harp will wake us in the mead-hall,

But ravens heavy from their eating
Will tell the eagles how they sported
When with the wolves they tore at corpses.

And that will be our last defeat,
For that will be the end of the Geats.
But for the remnant, something worse:
The exile-path, a wound that hurts
More than the path of spear through flesh.
You wander through the land—no rest,
No hall, no lord, no kin, no rights.
Death is better than shameful life."

Then he told one of them to take the news
To all the others waiting at a distance
Beyond the wood, wondering which to choose
As likely—life or death.
                              And their resistance
To death went down in tears: the rider's face,
Before his words, revealed his own disgrace

And so they knew that Beowulf was dead.
These watchers had less luck than those who'd stayed
By Hart or Grendel's pool. So now, instead
Of cheering, slowly one by one they strayed
Over the hill, to gaze upon the worst
Their fate could do. They found the dragon first.

Quickly they gathered round and stood amazed,
Staring; it lay some thirty feet stretched out,
Reddish-yellow, metallic, as if glazed
By years of lying against gold. Its snout,
With grinning jaws and horn-like teeth wide spaced,
Still dripped the fire that Beowulf had faced,

But now it fed on the monster's mouth and tongue
And licked up toward a staring goatish eye.
One man fingered a claw, another flung
His spear into its short plump chicken-thigh.
No more would it fly through midnight air, or lurk
In treasure-caves! A hero's handiwork,

The burnt-out carcass smoldered in the dirt.
And not far off, on higher ground, was he
Who fought the monster, now beyond all hurt.
Equal in death, those two; not equally
Beloved. The men, approaching, loudly cried
To see the lord who gave them rings—who died

The cairn on the headland is an ancient
landmark of Weder Island Fjord.

For them—so wholly helpless, like the dragon.
Wiglaf stood at his master's head and spoke:

"Look at his face, my friends; it soon will change,
Be gone forever. How those hands and arms,
Just now so quick with strength, are strange in stillness.
Yet he should not have died, not here and now!
We couldn't make the dear man heed our counsel
That he should let the guardian of that gold
Lie in the darkness where it long had lain,
Unseen, untouched, until the end of the world.
Fate was too strong for him—the highest fate
A man can have, like Sigmund's, son of Waels,
Who without help from Fitela, his friend
And son, had killed the dragon in the cave,
Nailing it with his sword against the wall;
He saw it melt in its heat, then stole its treasure.
So Beowulf. But we must take away
The treasure; he cannot. So hard his will,
So fixed his thoughts, he had to fight—and die.

He bid me greet you. Said to build a mound
Over the place we burn his body, a barrow
High and handsome, to suit a hero's life.

Now quick! I have such things to show,
Such wealth of twisted rings, thick gold,
Wonders behind that wall, that never,
For all your love of ancient treasure,
Will you have need again to see
So much, so close! And while we seek
Those riches, have a bier made ready
So we can bear our lord to heaven
When we come out; so we can take him
Where God will have his welcome waiting."

Then Wiglaf summoned seven men,
The best, to help him get the hoard,
And told the others to go out
To forests near or far with wagons
And bring in many cords of balewood.
"For now a flame full grown will feed
Ravenously upon our lord,
Whose fate had kept him from the feasting
Of wolves and crows, from being killed

The cairn with the fjord in the background.

When arrows showered over shieldwalls."
The men went out with mules and wagons,
Axes and heavy rope, and hewed,
And split, and lashed the logs together–
Trunks of the oldest, toughest oaks
And pines that oozed with heady pitch.
They heaped the flamewood high at Hron-ness,
Stacking it in a square-set shape
Beside the sudden drop to the sea.

Meanwhile Wiglaf, taking a torch, had led–
No need to force! –his men inside the mound,
None too sad that the treasure-guard was dead.
They carried outside everything they found
And piled a wain with the countless priceless things–
Armor and jewels, plate and twisted rings.

And then they had the dragon's funeral:
They shoved it over the cliff, and let the sea
Take it. Then set an oxen-team to haul
The creaking wain to Hron-ness. Reverently,
At last, they bore the king, all wrapped in fur,
To where the balewood and the treasure were.

Each laid his shield, or sharpest sword,
Or helm, or brightest byrnie down
Among the cross-hatched mass of logs;
And laid the body of Beowulf
Amidst the treasures of his men,
High atop the mountain of timber.
Then mourning warriors woke the flames;
Black smoke above the balefire rose
A flawless column–the air was calm.
And roaring mingled with the moaning,
Greatest of fires and greatest grief,
Breaking the hero's bonehouse, breaking
The hearts of all the hero's people.
But you could see one lady saddest
Of all, who sang the mourning-song,
Her grey hair bound, whom Beowulf
And Higelac alike had loved.
She wept for Beowulf, but also
It was herself she mourned for, seeing
The future years, and for the Geats:
The fall of slaughtered flesh, the hunger–
She was not Hildeburh with Hengest,
The Geats would have no home to go to,
They would be slaves, not people.
                              Slowly
Heaven swallowed the smoke, and cleared.

A view of the archipelago from the cairn at dusk.

The people built a barrow on the ashes—
Forty feet high, two hundred long; it loomed
Dark on the sky, and could be seen from far
By men on ships. Ten days it took to make.
Inside it were the bones of Beowulf
That men had cleaned and closed in a golden box;
And fire-leavings from the Geatish war-things;
And all the golden goods and gems and silver
Hidden long ago in the Hron-ness cave.
They left that hall-thanes' hoard for earth to hold,
Thinking that no one now had strength to wield it,
No one alive. As useless now to men
As it had always been, it lies deep buried.

Twelve men in armor rode around the barrow
Slowly through the gathering snow and darkness.
They sang of Beowulf, they wept his passing;
Said that of all the heroes under heaven
He was the mildest to his men; most loved
Among his people, kindest king; most eager
For worthy praise.

        All you who pass, remember:
Beowulf Ecgtheowsson is buried here.
The strongest and the best, yet still he died.

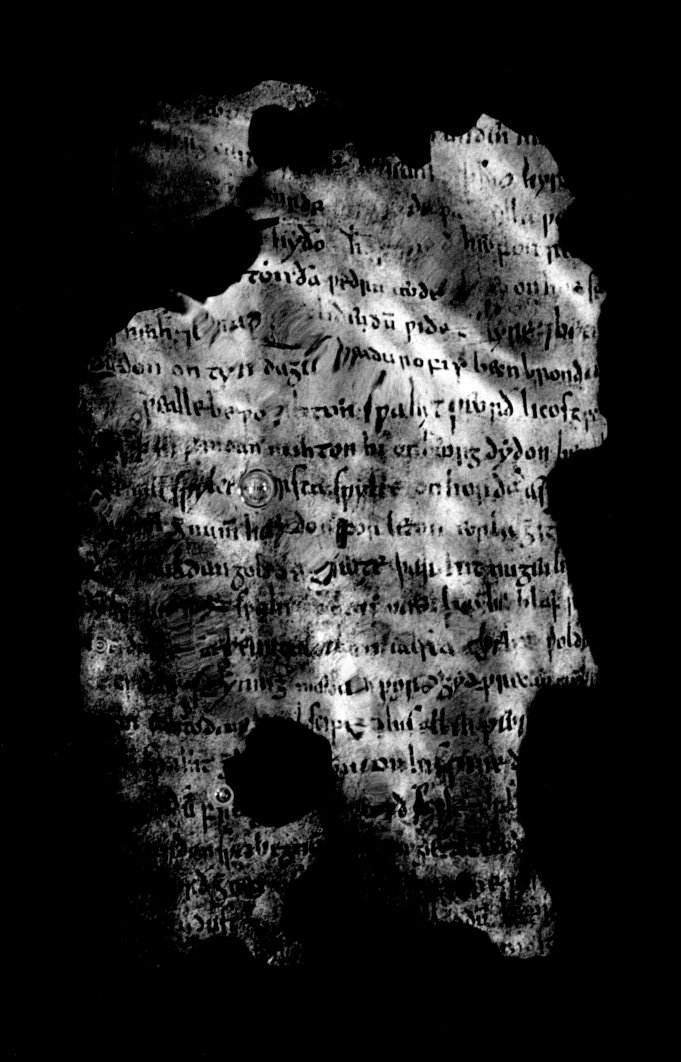

Standing stones near Fjällbacka

Glossary

bower: a small dwelling, like a cabin

byrnie: a coat or shirt of mail

millefiori: "a kind of ornamented glass made by fusing together a number of glass rods of different sizes and colours, and cutting the mass into sections" (Shorter OED)

nicor: a water-monster or -demon or -sprite

sax: a short sword, apparently typical of the "Saxons"

Scyldings: descendants of Scyld, i.e. Danes

Tiw: the principal war-god worshipped among heathen Anglo-Saxons, corresponding to Mars and giving us "Tuesday" (c.f. "mardi," Mars-day, French for Tuesday)

Weland: legendary smith famous throughout the ancient Germanic world

wes hael: Anglo-Saxon greeting, meaning literally "be whole, be healthy" and giving us "wassail"

Acknowledgments: I would like to thank the Humanities Research Institute at U.C. Berkeley for their support, and also the following persons: Ed and Linda Avak, who found the poem worth reading aloud; Leonard Cottrell, for inspiration long ago and again more recently; Barry Goldensohn, for his technical imprimatur; Thom Gunn, whose stringent metrical reading allowed me to see clearly what I was doing; John Hollander, for his strong support; Tia Kratins, as lively and sharp a reader as one could wish; George Ladd, for what he said about this poem; Rodney Merrill, for certain particulars; Bernice F. Oliver, for her firm and hopeful intuition; Marijane Osborn, for several dozen useful suggestions; Fred C. Robinson, who in the early months gave me faith in the public value of this project, saw its eventual shape, and has never ceased to sustain it with the strength of well-earned authority; Donald E. Stanford, my mentor for this and many other poems; Randolph Swearer, the master of ceremonies, who with rarest skill and tact has brought the whole thing about; and, as usual, for the lioness's share of help, Mary Anne Oliver.

Standing stones at Leire

Imagining the Real-World Setting of *Beowulf*

Marijane Osborn

Despite its monsters, the poem *Beowulf* displays a tendency toward realism, a tendency that I will explore in this commentary. I am here as scholar-voyager to take you through the images of our book on a journey into the world of the story. With emphasis upon place and artifacts rather than plot, we will go from the poet's England to Denmark, and then onward with the story to Wedermark, a less certain place on the map.

First, however, let me comment on the introductory sequence of images as an example of how each of the contributors to this book is interacting independently with the original *Beowulf*. Here the designer Randolph Swearer imitates one way that the Anglo-Saxon poet inserts a Christian subtext into the poem, even though the story is set in heathen Scandinavia before Christianity was brought to the North. The poet achieves a double worldview through a montage effect for which the Sutton Hoo helmet offers a metaphor. Very much as the poet manipulates his material in the original *Beowulf,* Randolph Swearer has manipulated an image of the magnificent pagan helmet found at Sutton Hoo in East Anglia to make it hint at Christian themes. The attentive viewer will observe that the helmet piece on page v literally represents a flying bird or dragon, a protective battle-creature that would seem entirely native to the people who made and wore it. But from our later perspective we can reinterpret this cross-shaped pagan object in terms of Christian symbolism, an act of interpretation that a sixth-century Scandinavian could not have performed. The poet's remarks to us about the monster Grendel's descent from Cain would have been equally incomprehensible to someone of Beowulf's own heathen world.

After Oliver's prologue and before the poem begins is a page from the original *Beowulf* manuscript, a text based on traditions of an earlier culture and perhaps based on earlier manuscripts as well. Shaped like the silhouette of a standing stone, this page marks the entrance to Beowulf's long ago Iron Age world. With the opening of the poem we tentatively enter that earlier world in the images.

Yeavering: p. 11

The landscape beneath the first lines of the poem is Yeavering in northern England, where the outline of an enormous Anglo-Saxon hall, probably belonging to the Northumbrian king Edwin (d. A.D. 633), was discovered beneath the meadow grass. In this desolate place only the faint mounds left by excavation mark the sites of long-ago buildings, once a complex settlement full of milling people. Today the wind blows over a bare field, with the high hill called Yeavering Bell looming darkly above. Though unseen in the photograph, a row of dead ravens hangs on a fence in the woods, the Northumbrian equivalent of a scarecrow. Their flapping feathers and the bawling sheep are the only things moving here, the only sound not of wind in the grass. Over this landscape, as empty now as it was before halls were thought of, the poem begins.

Sutton Hoo: pp. 12–13

The second landscape, beneath Scyld's spirit ship, is Sutton Hoo in East Anglia, far to the south of Yeavering. Here where the air smells of salt from the nearby sea, the trace of a ninety-foot-long rowing vessel was excavated in 1939, merely the ghost of a ship because its timbers had long since rotted away while the nails remained in place to reveal its contours. Carefully the excavators brushed away the clotted sands to disclose, in the bosom of the long ship, royal armor and other accoutrements, including fragments of a musical instrument—rich possessions for the prince to take with him to the other world. He even had a purseful of coins, perhaps for the ghostly oarsmen who would row him to that alien shore. The elegant and lavish treasures laid around Scyld at the beginning of *Beowulf* were once thought to be entirely a figment of the poet's romantic imagination. But the wealth of Scyld's ornate treasure ship was given credibility by the discovery of the solid real-world treasures buried in the seventh century at Sutton Hoo. Raymond Oliver has used these rich finds and others to re-imagine the poetic burial. Randolph Swearer has used this Anglo-Saxon landscape with its many still untouched mounds to evoke a long ago ancestral time as a setting for the death ship of Scyld.

In the sea-washed air above that rolling landscape of burial mounds there floats the distorted image of a vessel based on the ninth-century Scandinavian Oseberg ship. Its most startling feature is one that the Sutton Hoo ship did not possess: a coiled prow. Technically speaking, the ship with coiled prow that the original poet imagines for Scyld is an anachronism in the early world of the poem, because this stunning ship style seems not to have become popular before the late eighth century. Raymond Oliver, emphasizing the sixth-century world of the story, gives Scyld's ship a "hawk-beak prowhead," reflecting the gaping jaws of the animal-head stem posts on earlier Germanic ships (so magical that an old heathen law required incoming ships to turn these stem posts away from land in order not to disturb the land spirits). Perhaps the Anglo-Saxon poet was using the more contemporary coiled prow, along with other objects and customs, to give his poem a distinctive Scandinavian coloring, for he begins the poem by telling us that the story took place long ago among the Danes, then he reinforces that location almost at once by showing us an elegant and uniquely Scandinavian ship awaiting its sad cargo, the corpse of the Danish king. Through the photographer's ability both to record and to allude, Randolph Swearer intends to symbolize the way the English poet fuses realities of his own time and place with an ancient Scandinavian story.

When Scyld's descendant King Hrothgar comes to power, he builds a mighty hall and names it "Hart." Even when the lake of the monsters appears in dismal contrast, this golden hall dominates the Danish landscape of the first part of the poem. But in the images accompanying the poem we have not yet left the poet's England. In the reconstructed Anglo-Saxon village of West Stow, not far from Sutton Hoo, we finally encounter some life: re-bred Iron Age chickens and costumed villagers baking "Anglo-Saxon" bread, loaves that smell better than they taste. But in the next scenes, as we begin to move away from England, we are again in solitude, gazing through the ruined walls of Bamburgh Castle out over Lindisfarne, then through the planks of the West Stow buildings, moving past the traditionally carved post of a stave-church door—going back in time to "Heorot," the hall of the Hart.

"Meaning is in things," says our poet Oliver, and lavish and rich are the objects displayed inside the hall in his poem. In a tribal culture like this, the ceremonial hall is the focus of both memories and promise, embracing and giving significance to all that matters most. The Danes dedicate the newly built hall with a great banquet, unaware that their companionable words, lit with harpsong and laughter, will anger a wordless presence in the darkness outside. Yet they take precautions against

West Stow: p. 15

such dangers with a spell against the night (in Oliver's poem), and when the evil nevertheless bursts upon them they will sacrifice to the gods "at sacred well and tree." But in both the original and the modern poem they sacrifice more tamely than on those spectacular occasions reported near the Scylding stronghold by eleventh-century Thietmar of Merseburg. Though Thietmar's exaggerated hearsay about this practice has not been directly substantiated by archaeology, evidence of animal and even human sacrifice is found throughout Denmark, and animal heads warding off evil are represented on helmets, houses, and (as in Oliver's poem) ships' prows. The protective horse sacrifice at the reconstructed sacrificial bog near Gamle Leire in Denmark is heart-stopping to come upon unexpected amid the dark woods; it provides a visual analogy for the Danes' spell against the night. The photograph was taken at the outdoor museum in Herthadal, not far from where royal halls like Hrothgar's once stood. The bog is fetid with rotting trees, and the carcass is real, its skull pointing over the water.

Gamle Leire: pp. 22–23

But the Danes find little protection in either the hall or their charms against the night. When the monster comes, the image shows him emerging from the very pages of the manuscript itself, from the Anglo-Saxon book about monsters titled *The Marvels of the East,* which is bound together with the *Beowulf* poem. The violence of his depredations upon the helpless Danes makes Grendel famous, and far away a young warrior, determined to rid Hart Hall of its demon, prepares with a chosen group of companions to sail to Denmark.

Marvels of the East: p. 25

Hart Hall is usually imagined to be at Gamle Leire near Roskilde in northern Zealand; there Saxo Grammaticus, writing around A.D. 1200, situates the center of Scylding rule. As Beowulf and his men sail to the aid of the Scylding king Hrothgar, they must be coming south over that branch of the Baltic Sea called the Cattegat, west of Sweden, because they sail across open ocean until "the sea-cliffs glitter in the distance." If they were coming to the north coast of Zealand from Jutland or across the Öresund from southern Sweden, they would never leave sight of land. From the castle at Helsingør (Hamlet's Elsinore) on a bright day like that in the poem, the shore of Sweden, a mere three miles away, looks close enough to swim to. Only by sailing down from the north, perhaps along the coast to Falkenberg then by dead reckoning from there, would Beowulf and his men cross open sea until they encountered the Danish cliffs.

But these Danish cliffs have raised doubts. The "cliff that beetles o'er the sea" upon which Shakespeare perches Hamlet's castle is a notorious dramatization of the tame and low-lying coastline of that more easterly part of Zealand. Moreover, shining cliffs at the end of a sea-journey are part of a tradition dating back to Vergil, and they occur also in the Germanic type-scene where a gleam is followed by violence (as in Swearer's design the shining words of the reversed image of the manuscript anticipate violence in our book). Such analogues as Vergil and the Germanic type-scene have led scholars to believe that the seacliffs in *Beowulf* must be entirely fictional, a traditional motif rather than real topography. But this reasoning is faulty, for tradition and reality can coexist. It is a fact that if you sail for Roskilde Fjord from the open sea, the very first thing you will see is the long line of shining cliffs that mark the northern coast there. Rounding the cliffs one sails into Roskilde Fjord, a true "swan road" where swans really glide, leading deep into the land, to Leire.

Having landed and satisfied the coast guard about their intentions,

Beowulf and his Wedergeat companions march across the wild country-side until they can see Hart Hall. The poet emphasizes the magnificence of this royal Scylding hall, and in recent years the Roskilde archaeologist Tom Christensen has excavated, right at Gamle Leire, traces of a huge hall approximately the size of an Olympic swimming pool. But this real Leire Hall is later than fictional Hart, perhaps even of the poet's own period. Since the main evidence for Leire Hall is its postholes, now reburied, we have based the idea of Hrothgar's hall upon the reconstructed Viking Age hall at Trelleborg, another large Danish hall that like Leire Hall was built nearer to the poet's time than to Beowulf's. Though the exterior of this hall has now been reinterpreted without the porch, both its more accurate interior and its dimensions may be used to evoke Hart Hall, imagined here brand-new and still smelling of freshly worked timber. When Beowulf arrives at the carved doorway, however, it is seasoned and slightly neglected after years under attack. On this tribal threshold, where identity matters most, he declares himself: *Beowulf is min nama.*

Despite Hrothgar's warm welcome, when Beowulf announces in Hart Hall his intention of fighting Grendel, the king's adviser Unferth rudely challenges him with a story apparently of failure in a swimming race. In response to that challenge Beowulf gives another version of the swimming match with Breca. It is a tale of boyish recklessness and courage set in his own land. One of the names in his story, because it makes clearer the northern location of that homeland, is important for us here. Breca comes to shore in the land of the Heatho-*Reamas,* a tribal name that suggests proximity to the Swedish-Norwegian border river now called Glomma, then apparently called Raum, a Scandinavian form of the Old English name element *Ream.* Beowulf, after winning the match with Breca and also making the waters safe for seafarers by killing some monsters who haunt it, lands stormtossed on his own wooded shores not far south (this is my own unorthodox interpretation). As he retells the story on the eve before his fight, his point is to reassure Hrothgar's people about his stamina and his monster-killing, not his swimming. The *poet* may have an additional purpose, to prepare us for Beowulf's later swim down into Grendel's mere.

As he relates the Breca story, Beowulf peers out through the Sutton Hoo helmet, the helmet from which the protective flying bird of the title page was taken. This page reflects Randolph Swearer's fascination with entrances and passageways, and also the layers of history, recollection, and interpretation that pervade *Beowulf* and Raymond Oliver's re-shaping of it. On other occasions Randolph Swearer suggests this layering of perspective and time by use of the manuscript as a design element, but here he uses the frame of the helmet to suggest an "interior space" in which Beowulf recalls past events. The young hero relives these events in words, spoken words represented here by the manuscript text.

Later that night after the banquet, as the Geats are left to guard the hall, only Beowulf remains alert. We anticipate Grendel's coming from the same perspective that Beowulf does, as the very idea of the monster falls like a shadow across the hall and across the gleaming poem. Then the point of view is Grendel's as he approaches the hall, his fiery eyes lit with anticipation, seeing and yet not quite seeing the glint of a helmet awaiting him. The encounter is violent but brief, and afterwards nothing remains of the monster in Hart Hall except for his torn-off arm, set up in the crossed gable beams that arc against the sky. The next morning the hall is cleaned and repaired after the bloody fight, and the carved beams polished. Tapestries, or more properly story-strip embroideries, are hung along the wall like colorful bunting as the Danes prepare for a huge celebration that night. But it will be a night of surprises.

For Grendel's mother comes. The Danes had not known she existed. Coming to avenge her son, she strikes in the hall that night as the warriors sleep after the banquet, and vanishes almost before they can wake up. Her victim is Aescher, the king's best friend. In wicked heathen fashion she leaves his severed head in the path to her lair to unnerve the foes she knows will follow her. Perhaps she stakes it on a pole like the horse sacrifice in the woods, and points it at them, warding them off.

Olaus Wurmius's Leire map: p. 67

When they come upon this distressing and eerie sight, the Danes and Geats have pursued Grendel's mother where real landscape blends into myth. Olaus Wurmius's 1643 prospect of Leire represents the topographic reality which the earlier historian Saxo Grammaticus associated with the Scylding dynasty. A romantic ninetenth-century German scholar named Sarrazin proposed that the story landscape between Hart Hall and Grendel's pool was based upon this real topography from Gamle Leire to the Kattinge Sø (then an inlet from the fjord, now an independent lake). Where large stones are set in the shape of a ship on a hilltop bright with wildflowers, we participate in Sarrazin's fantasy, looking north across the gently undulating meadows toward the monster's abode.

If the Anglo-Saxon poet was working with this tranquil landscape either from personal knowledge or from hearsay, he elaborated it beyond all recognition. Mainly he added Gothic horrors from sermons about Hell, thus sharing in a particularly English tradition of a northern Hell-lake inhabited by a female demon or ghost. Perhaps a Celtic pond-deity (like King Arthur's beneficent Lady of the Lake), Scandinavian waterfall trolls, and monastic visions of the netherworld as Hell all come together here to produce Grendel's mother in her watery home, a lake overhung with hoary trees and aswim with strange demonic creatures in its fiery depths.

Whatever the ancestry of the monster and her lake in the world of story, her vicious attack on Hart Hall must be avenged. Once again Beowulf pledges to win or die, and armed with the sword that Unferth urges upon him he plunges into the stagnant waters. Unferth's sword fails him when he fights the troll-woman far down in the depths of the lake, and Beowulf casts it aside. Then light falls on a sword made by giants, more suitable for a hero's swing. Flashing like an icicle on fire, the fantasy sword brandished in the image is a construction made from the engraving of an Anglo-Saxon hilt and a manufactured blade, a blade clearly ready to flare and melt in the demon blood, as does that of the giant sword of the underwater cave.

Anglo-Saxon sword hilt: p. 69

On his victorious return Beowulf is honored appropriately by Hrothgar's words and his treasure, two resources of a great king. On the following morning he and his Geats take their leave. As the images on the next few pages take him home, we may imagine more precisely where that home lies.

The poem indicated earlier that Beowulf's homeland lies within two days' good sailing from Gamle Leire, perhaps north on the Swedish coast beyond modern Gothenburg. In our voyage of the imagination we locate Wedermark where the coastal village of Fjällbacka lies between Gothenburg and Oslo. Though at the limits of possibility in terms of sailing time, this location is enhanced by such local antiquities as the discovery at nearby Hög Edsten of a Frankish sword pommel of garnet and gold, almost identical to the garnet and gold pommel found at Sutton Hoo. This

Väderöfjord map: p. 77

The ship "Ror Ege": p. 79

discovery provides a geographical link that *Beowulf* voyagers may find attractive. There is also the name of the district itself, *Väderöfjord,* "Weder Island Fjord"; whether or not it is coincidence, this name is appropriate for the homeland of Beowulf's Wedergeats. Therefore our spiral prow approaches the archipelago on that coast. The next scene places us aboard the reconstructed Viking Age ship, the Roar Ege ("Hrothgar's Oak"), modelled on a ship found in Roskilde Fjord and probably truer to the ship a sixth-century warrior would have sailed in than the poet's ship with spiral prow. Ahead of us are the rocky formations that we imagine the homecoming Wedergeats seeing hundreds of years ago. We wind through this labyrinth of rocks protecting the harbor, and coming into that harbor we pass under the shadow of a mountainous rock that truly does "beetle"—like the *beorg* or "brooding cliff" beneath which Beowulf leaped aboard his boat to set out on his adventure.

If the landscape of Gamle Leire seemed innocent and open (though secreting that sacrificial bog in a fold in the nearby woods), this harsher landscape, darkly brooding and dense with Bronze Age rock carvings, dares us to wrest away its mysteries. This impression is partly a product of the unusual land formations typical of the area, long humps of glacier-wrought granite-like rocky islands afloat amid forests, with fertile cultivated fields stretched out between on flatlands that a few millennia ago were seabeds. In fact, it is just this pattern of granite outcroppings that continues out into the fjord to give us the dangerous but protective archipelago of islands. Weder Island Fjord has been so named, I have been told, because here the wildest storms in Sweden sweep in directly from the North Sea. But it is calm weather as we navigate in to shore, and the land welcomes us with a little sheltered cove, pink with blossoming sea thrift against the embracing granite.

Locating Wedermark here would make the Wedergeats of *Beowulf* a separate and vulnerable northern branch of those Geats or Gautar who ruled in southern Sweden. Whether this is the true Wedermark, or whether Wedermark ever existed, both the natural features of this area and its abundance of Iron Age antiquities encourage us to use it as a stage-set for the rest of the poem. We imagine the hall of Beowulf's peo-

Stave church door: p. 81

ple, represented by the image of another stave church door, set on a rise not far from our landing place. On this west-facing shore the hall faces south to protect it from the wild seawinds, and on this clear day the afternoon sunlight makes the bright, pale wood of the hall seem almost ablaze. At home, Beowulf relates his Danish adventure to his uncle and king, Higelac, and through the "eyes" of the Sutton Hoo helmet we reflect upon these events from his interior space. But after telling his king about the monster fights, Beowulf displays his sense of audience by assessing the political situation he observed in the Danish royal hall: The gold-bedecked princess Freawaru, pledged to marry to settle a feud, is doomed to fail in her peace-weaving. It is probably in the renewal of that feud that Hart Hall is destined to be burned down.

But we do not see this hall-burning in the poem. In *Beowulf* it is not the Hart Hall familiar to us but the Geatish hall in Wedermark that burns, many years later, in a disaster that no one could have foreseen. After Beowulf's king Higelac has died in a Frisian raid, and Beowulf, having slain the Frankish warrior who killed his king, returns to Wedermark—perhaps bearing a colorful Frankish sword like that of Hög Edsten as his trophy—he is made regent, then after further battles, king. He has ruled for fifty years when a fire-dragon disturbed in its den rages forth upon the land, and the royal hall of Wedermark vanishes in flames.

Burning *Beowulf*
manuscript: pp. 94–99

In the images, flames eat the pages of the poem itself, pages that have in fact been damaged both by fire and by time. Here I want to intrude a personal response to the images. When I first saw them I was deeply shocked, perhaps as the Geats were by seeing their hall destroyed, for much of my life is in this poem and the photographs are convincingly real. My response was strengthened by an awareness that this unique manuscript of *Beowulf* was very nearly lost to fire in real life, before any other copy of it existed. It was kept in the unluckily-named Ashburnham House, which caught fire in 1731. The manu-script, though singed, was saved. It has suffered since from crumbling edges (as may be seen in the silhouette-shapes throughout this book), but we may be thankful that it was not destroyed like the hall of the Wedergeats. With that hall gone, the only "place" remaining in the mysterious land of the poem is the dragon's lair, hidden beyond the scope of either the design or my commentary. There Beowulf must again go to do battle, and in winning, die. The mood grows darker. Images fail.

Yet the hero's death does not mark the end of the world of the poem. Before dying of the poisonous wound inflicted by the dragon, he has asked for his people to remember him with a beacon built in his honor, "high and handsome, to suit a hero's life," for remembrance is immortality in this pagan world. But Beowulf in his dying speech, thinking as so often of the common good, has specified something else as well. He has asked that his memorial be "a mound atop the headland" which seafarers will associate with his name and take their bearings from, perhaps in making their way through the rocky passage into this safe harbor. These words strike me as highly allegorical as I write them, but anyone who has navi-gated that sea-lashed, skerry-studded fjord will recognize the practical need for such landmarks. These two impulses of allegory and realism resonate together throughout the story, for as the Anglo-Saxon maxim assures us, "Every man's life is another man's lore."

The cairn at Fjällbacka: pp. 108–113

In the final images, we see the funeral fire on the hilltop and the rocks of the cairn overlooking the fjord as it stretches away west past the Weder Islands into the evening seas. Even as the great Hart Hall rises to em-brace and celebrate a heroic way of life in the first part of *Beowulf,* pyre and beacon memorialize a single hero's life in the last part of the poem, as an age draws to a close. Once the praises are sung, even the fire must die, and we are told that the people themselves, surrounded on all sides by ancient enemies, must now disperse. Yet at the end of the poem, when the halls are gone, the fire burning low, and the Wedergeats doomed, there still stands in memory of their hero that high and generous cairn above the sea—and the poem itself.

Submerged *Beowulf*
manuscript page: p. 115

Acknowledgments: In addition to acknowledging here the sensitive and supportive readings that each of the contributors to this volume has offered me, I should like to note my particular gratitude to my dear friend Carol Martin, who encouraged me to go on my first "Beowulf-ian" voyage and arranged for the little yacht upon which we sailed, to Peter Bolwig who captained us, to Gillian Overing for being my com-panion on that first trip and for obtaining a grant toward expenses from Wake Forest University, to Randolph Swearer for a second journey (by land) and for this opportunity to integrate that journey into a larger pro-ject, and to the Regents of the University of California for grants that have contributed to explorations of this kind for several summers.

The mid-ninth-century seal
of the bishop of Dunwich

Colophon

Beowulf: A Likeness is designed by Randolph Swearer and published by Yale University Press. The book was printed by Rembrandt Printing, Woodbridge, Connecticut, in an edition of 3,000 copies. Typesetting is by Highwood Typographic Services. The text paper is 80lb Lustro Offset dull. The contrasting typefaces used in this volume are Univers, designed by Swiss typographer Adrian Frutiger in the 1950s, and Bembo, which is based on a typeface designed by Francesco Griffo of Bologna for Aldus Manutius in 1495. Frutiger's Univers is inspired by the integrated family of nineteenth-century fonts Akzidenz Grotesque by the firm of Bethold. The structure and style of Bembo are influenced by Griffo's interest in pre-Carolingian script forms.

The following organizations have generously granted permission to use illustrative material: The Trustees of the British Museum, The Sutton Hoo Research Project, The Early English Text Society, The British Library, The Society of Antiquaries of London, Rosenkilde Bagger Publishers, and The Institute of Archaeology, Art History, and Numismatics, University of Oslo.

Unless listed below, all photography and other illustrative material is by Randolph Swearer.

The *Beowulf* manuscript pages throughout this volume are reproduced by permission of the British Library and the Early English Text Society from: Julius Zupitza (ed.), *Beowulf (Facsimile)* (Early English Text Society No. 245.) 2d edition. London: Oxford University Press, 1959. Page v: adaptation of Sutton Hoo helmet by RS from British Museum photograph; p. ix: adaptation of Sutton Hoo helmet bird ornament by RS from British Museum photograph; pp. 12–13: Sutton Hoo landscape, Kate Breakey; p. 15: West Stow photograph, Kate Breakey; p. 21: stave church door frame from Du Chaillu, *The Viking Age,* New York: Charles Scribner's Sons, 1890; pp. 22–23: photograph of Leire bog, Kate Breakey; p. 25: adaptation of headless man illustration by RS from: Kemp Malone (ed.) *The Nowell Codex* (Early English Manuscripts in Facsimile, No. 12) Copenhagen: Rosenkilde Bagger Publishers, 1963; pp. 26, 28–29: RS's photographs of the Oseberg Ship by special permission of The Institute of Archaeology, Art History, and Numismatics, University of Oslo; pp. 32–33 Trelleborg Hall photograph, Kate Breakey; p. 43 adaptation of Sutton Hoo helmet by RS from British Museum photograph; pp. 50–51: circular croppings of Sutton Hoo helmet adapted by RS from British Museum photograph; pp. 63, 65: creatures adapted by RS from Kemp Malone (ed.) *The Nowell Codex;* p. 67: map of Leire from Olaus Wurmius, *Danicorum Monumentorum,* 1643, by courtesy of the Beinecke Rare Book and Manuscript Library, Yale University; p. 69: sword handle from *Archaeologia* No. 30, London: Society of Antiquities, 1844; p. 77: map by Treaty Oak Press with RS; p. 81: door of stave church from Du Chaillu, *The Viking Age;* p. 83: Sutton Hoo helmet adapted by RS from British Museum photograph; pp. 104–07: background flames by RS and Kate Breakey; spears from Du Chaillu, *The Viking Age;* pp. 108–13, 118: landscape photographs by Kate Breakey; p. 126: Anglo-Saxon stamp from *Archaeologia,* no. 20, London.